Wives – Mothers – Daughters – Widows

CORNISH WOMEN IN THE CARIBBEAN

From the 17th to the 19th Centuries

WIVES – MOTHERS
DAUGHTERS – WIDOWS

CORNISH WOMEN
in the
CARIBBEAN

From the 17th to the 19th Centuries

Sue Appleby

Copyright © 2024 Sue Appleby

The moral right of the author has been asserted.

Unless otherwise noted, all images used in
this publication are in the Public Domain

Apart from any fair dealing for the purposes of research or private study, or criticism or review, as permitted under the Copyright, Designs and Patents Act 1988, this publication may only be reproduced, stored or transmitted, in any form or by any means, with the prior permission in writing of the publishers, or in the case of reprographic reproduction in accordance with the terms of licences issued by the Copyright Licensing Agency. Enquiries concerning reproduction outside those terms should be sent to the publishers.

Troubador Publishing Ltd
Unit E2 Airfield Business Park,
Harrison Road, Market Harborough,
Leicestershire. LE16 7UL
Tel: 0116 2792299
Email: books@troubador.co.uk
Web: www.troubador.co.uk

ISBN 978-1-80514-373-4

British Library Cataloguing in Publication Data.
A catalogue record for this book is available from the British Library.

Printed and bound by CPI Group (UK) Ltd, Croydon, CR0 4YY
Typeset in 12pt Adobe Jenson Pro by Troubador Publishing Ltd, Leicester, UK

For Meiling and Sarah
Two Daughters of Independent Spirit

Contents

Foreword		ix
Acknowledgements		xi
Introduction		xv
1.	There is Great Want of Servants	1
2	Ladies of Quality	23
3	The Middling Sort	56
4	'Dear Sister': Wesleyan Methodist Missionary Women	91
5	Mining Women	115
	Bibliography	145
	Index	161

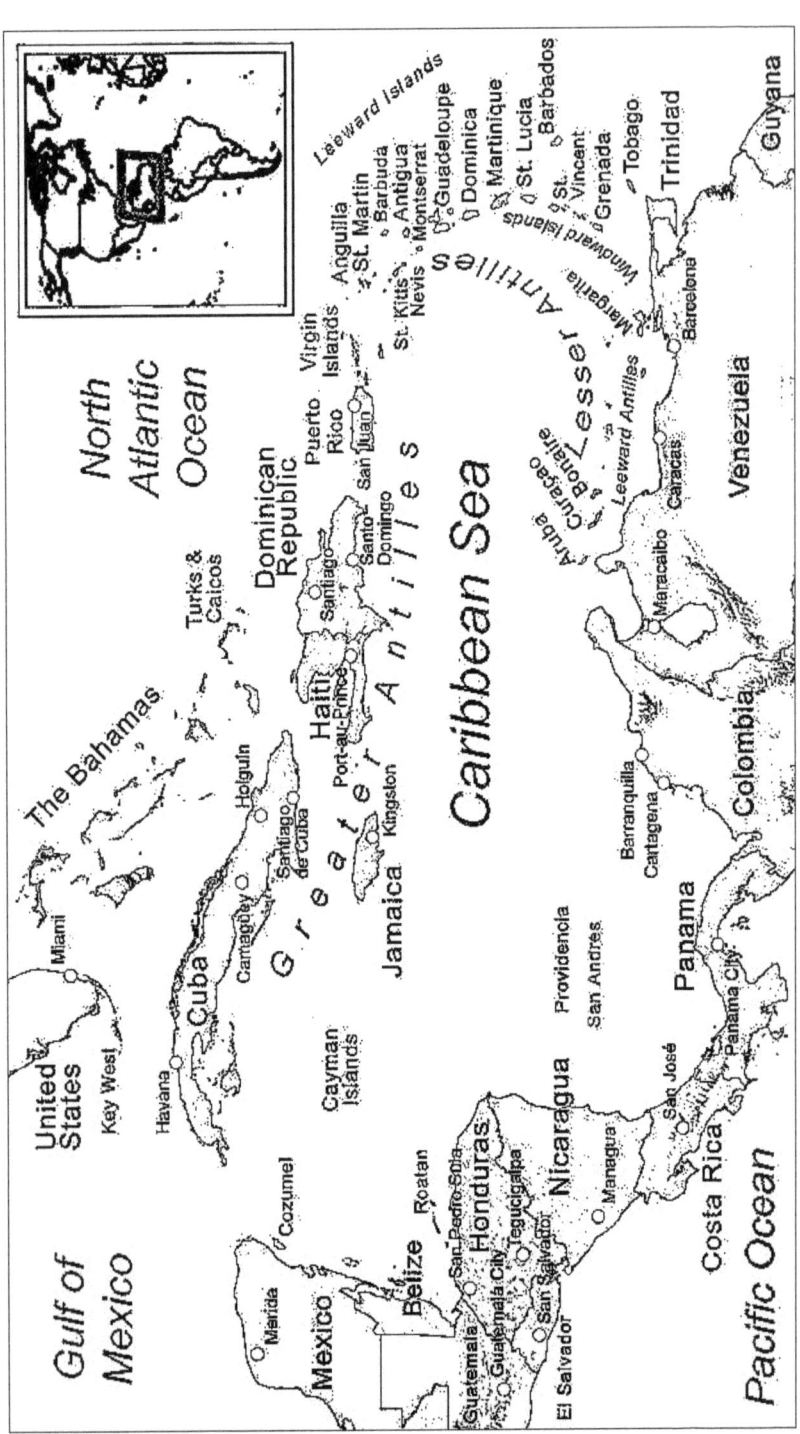

Foreword

Cornwall, that independently minded peninsula in the far south-west of Britain, with its distinctive character and now-recognised minority ethnicity, has for centuries been the source of migrants to all parts of the world. This has generated a broad literature on Cornish emigration and the Cornish abroad – the Cornish Diaspora – much of it concentrated on the better-known destinations of the USA, Australia, and South Africa, and almost all related to the international mining industry of the 19th century. But the Cornish went just about everywhere, and in her previous book on the topic Sue Appleby filled a geographical gap in that coverage by focusing on the Cornish in the Caribbean, reminding us that while mining was an important driver for migration there were other reasons why the Cornish left their homeland.

In the same way that the story of emigration from Cornwall has been dominated by mining, it has been dominated by men and their stories. In this new book, Appleby breaks the mould again, this time by examining the lives of the women from Cornwall who spent time in the Caribbean, voluntarily or otherwise. From indentured servants through the wives of mariners, miners, and missionaries, to the 'Middling Sort', and the 'Ladies of Quality' who joined their husbands on the great plantations, these women had many different reasons for travelling to the various islands of the Caribbean.

As Appleby writes, to research these women is 'a challenge', something I can heartily endorse from my own experience examining the lives of the wives of migrant miners. Nevertheless, by digging deep into the archives and preserved family histories, this author has revealed the fascinating stories and experiences of women whose lives and contributions would otherwise have remained footnotes in history.

There has in recent years been a gathering tide of research and literature into the lives of Cornish women. This much-needed development has seen publications and projects exploring women's work in Cornwall in industries from mining to textiles, and raising awareness of overlooked female contributions to literature, arts, sciences, politics, and social reform, as well to the musical and cultural life of Cornwall. Thus far, less work has concentrated on the women of the Cornish diaspora itself, so this new book is a very welcome addition to that literature.

Dr Lesley Trotter
Honorary Research Fellow
Institute of Cornish Studies
University of Exeter

Acknowledgements

The history of the 17th, 18th, and 19th centuries was largely written by men, and those men seldom considered women as worthy of research. While some women of the period, in particular 'Ladies of Quality'[1] and women of the 'Middling Sort', penned travel reminiscences, diaries, and – often voluminous – letters, very few of these were published. This meant that researching these women was something of a challenge for me. To research indentured female servants – who were most likely illiterate – and female members of Wesleyan Methodist missionary and mining families – whose words were almost never recorded – was even more of a challenge. To source information specifically about Cornish women who went to the Caribbean was the most challenging of all, and it is only with the help I received from the following people that I have been able to complete this book.

When I was researching indentured servants, Nicola Hole from the Bristol Archives assisted me in sourcing the names of some of the Cornish women who left from Bristol, and Victoria O'Flaherty, retired archivist of the National Archives in St Christopher, provided

---

1   The phrase 'Ladies of Quality' is taken from the title of Janet Schaw's book: *Journal of a Lady of Quality: Being the Narrative of a Journey from Scotland to the West Indies, North Carolina and Portugal, in the Years 1774 to 1776.*

valuable information on the background history of St Christopher and Nevis – islands where many of those indentured in the 17th century were sent.

As I looked for information about Cornish Ladies of Quality, Ian Mitchell assisted me by sharing his family research concerning Mary Elizabeth Bryan, and as I moved on to the Middling Sort, Elizabeth Shannon at the Wellin Museum of Art at Hamilton College, Clinton, New York, along with Maxine Symons and Kyle Scott, provided details about the life of Elizabeth Wingfield and her family, while Geoffrey Mann shared information about Jane Wright, the ship captain's wife.

Irene Robinson, the Revd Jenny Dyer, and John Lenton, Honorary Librarian of the Wesley Historical Society, provided me with sources which proved extremely useful as I researched the wives and daughters of Cornish Wesleyan Methodist missionaries, and Michelle Myburgh shared information from her family research about Methodist missionary wife Emily Hales.

At the beginning of my research into mining women, Lesley Trotter helped me to source Cornish mining families who had children born in the Caribbean, and Bill Curnow's detailed research into his ancestors' experiences in Jamaica and Cuba provided me with an insight into the lives of Cornish mining women living in the Caribbean that I would not have found elsewhere. Later in my research, Di Donovan, Ross Garner, Graham Lambert, Martin Wolfgang, and Lairg Parish all shared information about Cornish members of their families who went out to Caribbean mines, while John Heath, Online Parish Clerk (Genealogy) for Redruth, Mawnan, Mawgan in Meneage, and St Martin in Meneage, Cornwall, helped me solve the mystery of Mary Annear's maiden name. When the first draft of my manuscript was complete, Peter Moll read the section

ACKNOWLEDGEMENTS

that focuses on the Virgin Gorda copper mine and made some useful comments.

Angela Broome and Emily Goddard at the Courtney Library in Truro; the volunteers at the Cornwall Family History Society, also in Truro; Kim Cooper and the library and archive staff at Kresen Kernow in Redruth; and the staff at the Morrab Library in Penzance have all been of tremendous help to me at various times during this project.

Caroline Petherick has done her usual expert job of copy-editing my manuscript – the third book she has edited for me[2] – while the team at Troubador Publishing have guided me smoothly through the publication process.

Finally, a special thank you to Bridget Brereton, Professor Emerita of History at the St Augustine Campus of the University of the West Indies, Trinidad, and to Lesley Trotter, Honorary Research Fellow at the Institute of Cornish Studies, University of Exeter, Cornwall Campus, both of whom read through early drafts of my manuscript, made valuable comments concerning the accuracy of the information I researched, gave me useful additions to my list of resource documents, and made suggestions that greatly improved my grasp of the role of Cornish women in the Caribbean.

Sue Appleby
Antigua, 2023

---

[2] The other two are *The Cornish in the Caribbean: From the 17th to 19th Centuries* and *The Hammers of Towan: A Nineteenth-Century Cornish Family*.

Introduction

It was while reading Lesley Trotter's book *The Married Widows of Cornwall: The Story of the Wives 'Left Behind' by Emigration* that I began to think about the Cornish women who, instead of being left behind, went – either alone, or with husbands or family – to wherever a work opportunity beckoned, or marital responsibility demanded. It sparked in me an interest to research and write about these women who, whether for life or for a few years, made the Caribbean their home.

Historical documents and reports of events of national importance often fail to mention women's names, let alone describe their experiences and any impact they had on the lives of others, so in order for me to research and write about Cornish women in the Caribbean I had to utilise an eclectic range of resources. These included family histories not written for publication, journals, diaries, letters, archival Cornish and Caribbean newspaper articles, Census information, and details of Wesleyan Methodist missionary reports.

Cornish women from a range of social classes went to the Caribbean during the 17th, 18th, and 19th centuries. Girls from poor families went as indentured servants in the early days of colonial expansion. Ladies of Quality either married into the families of wealthy West Indian sugar planters with vast estates and went out to live on their plantations, or accompanied husbands who were appointed to senior posts in the colonial service. Women of the Middling Sort went independently to make a new life for themselves, or joined a husband employed in a mid-level administrative post – such as a plantation manager – or sailed with a husband who captained a ship which traded throughout the Caribbean. Young Cornish Wesleyan Methodist women left home to marry Cornish missionaries based in the Caribbean, and travelled with them as they were appointed to different islands every few years. Poorer women, from the St Austell area in particular, accompanied their husbands to the copper mine on the island of Virgin Gorda, where they were employed as surface workers, while others went out to the copper mines of Cuba, where their husbands worked as miners, mine agents, and mine captains.

These women lived in a patriarchal society when it was generally believed that men and women should inhabit a gender-based ideology which stated that there was a public sphere of government, politics, and business – the world of men – and a private or home-based domestic sphere, where women belonged. Men were independent, while women were dependent on men. Physically and intellectually, men were thought to be strong and superior, while women were thought to be weak and inferior; although morally, women were believed to be superior to men and were therefore expected to be pure in word and deed. For men, whether married or single, sex was central to their existence, but women existed to marry, and to produce and bring up children – preferably male – and often spent their fertile years in an almost constant state of pregnancy, a condition which made great demands on their health and well-being. As I hope I show in the following chapters, many of these Cornish women who went out to the Caribbean demonstrated to a varying degree – as did

INTRODUCTION

the 'wives left behind' – a self-confidence and spirited independence very different from the subservient behaviour expected of them by contemporary society.

Sue Appleby
Antigua, 2023

1

There Is Great Want of Servants

As the *Robert Bonaventure* sailed out of Plymouth Harbour on a cold February day in 1634, she carried thirty-three men, many from Cornwall, and two Cornish women: Ellin Nancarro and Jane Trewin. All were bound for the Caribbean island of St Christopher, all were indentured servants, and all – including Ellin and Jane – were recorded as: 'husbandmen bound to serve there some three and some four years.'[1] In England in the Middle Ages and early modern period a husbandman was a free tenant farmer or a small landowner, but in the context of indentured servitude a husbandman was an agricultural labourer. Most agricultural labourers were male, but in the early days of the servant trade, while female servants usually undertook domestic tasks, some were put to weed crops and do other general work on the plantation.[2] As husbandmen, Ellin and Jane were destined to join one of these groups of women.

---

1   Hotten, John Camden. *The Original List of Persons of Quality: Emigrants, Religious Exiles, Political Rebels. Serving Men Sold for a Term of Years, Apprentices, Children Stolen, Maidens Pressed, and Others. Who went from Great Britain to the American Plantations, 1600–1700*. London: Empire State Book Company, 1874, pp.152–153. Accessed 29 August 2021, https://babel.hathitrust.org/cgi/pt?id=mdp.39015003632877&view=1up&seq=9&skin=2021

2   Beckles, Hilary MacDonald. 'White Labour in Black Slave Plantation Society and Economy: A Case Study of Indentured Labour in Seventeenth Century Barbados.' PhD diss., University of Hull, 1980, p.56.

An Immigrant Ship of the Period Leaving Plymouth Harbour. From: Sawyer, J. D. and W. E. Griffis. History of the Pilgrims and Puritans, their Ancestry and Descendants. New York: Century History Company, 1922, p.274.

Born in 1614, Ellin Nancarro was twenty years old when she signed her indenture. She came from the ancient market town of Penryn, on the south coast of Cornwall, which during Ellin's youth was a lively and prosperous port and trading centre, handling quantities of tin, copper, and fish. But if Ellin made the decision to become an indenture servant of her own free will, she had perhaps decided that life in Penryn offered her few opportunities. Jane Trewin, meanwhile, was born in 1608, signed her indenture when she was twenty-six and, although Trewin is a Cornish surname, came from Plympton in Devon. Plympton was a stannary town,[3] an important trading centre

---

3   A stannary town was the administrative centre for the local collection of the tin coinage tax, the proceeds of which were passed to the Crown or, in Cornwall, to the

for locally mined tin, and miners from Jane's family probably crossed the border from Cornwall into Devon to earn a living in one of the local tin mines. Both women made their way to Plymouth and, like thousands of others, boarded a ship in the harbour which would take them far from home.

England had introduced the system of indentured servitude to provide much-needed labour for her new Atlantic colonies, and from soon after the establishment of Jamestown settlement in North America in 1607 until about the middle of the 18th century – when indentured servants had largely been replaced by enslaved workers brought from Africa – some 320,000 people from England, Wales, Scotland, Ireland, and Europe, were indentured, sailing to the colonies from the English ports of Bristol, London, Liverpool, and Plymouth. More than half went to serve in the Chesapeake colonies of Virginia and Maryland, a few went to Pennsylvania and other North American colonies, and about 35 per cent went to the Caribbean, most, to the Leeward Islands of St Christopher, Nevis, Antigua, and Montserrat, and to Barbados and Jamaica.[4]

The term 'indenture' comes from the physical appearance of a written legal contract made between two people. Once signed by both parties, the contract was cut in two using a jagged, or 'indentured', pattern. One half was held by each of the parties to the agreement, and in the case of any future challenge regarding the authenticity of the contract the first step was to submit the two halves of the written contract to see if the indentures of both parts of the document fitted together. If they did, this made it more likely that the contract was as originally agreed and had not been altered to the benefit of either party.

It is thought that about one quarter of the servants who crossed

---

4   Suranyi, Anna. *Indentured Servitude: Unfree Labour and Citizenship in the British Colonies*. Montreal: McGill-Queen's University Press, 2021, p.16.

the Atlantic to England's Caribbean colonies were female, most of them aged under forty. Statistics for the number of female servants shipped are incomplete, but of 836 sent to Barbados in 1634, 46 were female, while of the 1,159 who left London for the Caribbean between 1683 and 1686, 271 were female.[5] These women left few records of their servitude, partly because they were more likely to be illiterate than male servants and were therefore less likely to write about their experiences.[6]

Most servants had made a choice to be indentured; often impoverished, they would have seen the arrangement as an opportunity to make a new start and to improve their standard of living. Prospective servants were contracted by recruiting agents who competed for business at each port from which servants were shipped, and once the indenture was signed the agent was responsible for clothing and feeding the servant and paying for their passage. To make a profit, the agent had to make sure the length of indenture sold at the servant's destination would cover his costs and provide him with a reasonable profit margin, so the length of an indenture would be set according to the profit the agent wished to make.[7]

Some servants would have been forcibly indentured. Among their number were vagrants, who were generally considered as lazy good-for-nothings and a financial burden to their parish, and criminals who had successfully bargained for transportation to one of the

---

5   Shepherd, Verene (ed.) *Women in Caribbean History*. Kingston: Ian Randle, 2012, p.27.

6   Suranyi, Anna. 'Willing to Go if They Had Their Clothes: Early Modern Women and Indentured Servitude.' In *Challenging Orthodoxies: The Social and Cultural Worlds of Early Modern Women; Essays Presented to Hilda L. Smith*, eds. Sigrun Haude and Melinda S. Zook, pp.193–210. Abingdon: Routledge, 2016, p.193.

7   Galenson, David W. 'British Servants and the Colonial Indenture System in the Eighteenth Century.' *The Journal of Southern History*, pp.41–66 (Vol.44, No. 1,1978), pp.54–55.

colonies rather than accept the death penalty or a long period of imprisonment. Some were prisoners of war, including Royalists taken during the English Civil Wars (1642–1651) by Oliver Cromwell's forces, and rebel supporters of the Duke of Monmouth who had been imprisoned after the failure of the Monmouth Rebellion in 1685.

Some unfortunates were simply kidnapped and trafficked on board ship by individuals known as 'Spirits', who were experts at the:

> *carrying and stealing away [of] boyes maides and other persons and transporting them beyond the seas... without any knowledge or notice of the parents or others that have the care and oversight of them.*[8]

The government of the day did little to control the activities of the Spirits because although kidnapping was illegal there was a 'great want of servants'[9] in the colonies. Planters and merchants regularly sent requests to the government to supply servants in greater numbers, and even when Spirits were caught they were sometimes allowed to continue shipping out their captured servants.

The objective of the ships' captains was to take the largest number of servants to their destination as quickly and cheaply as possible, and as many servants as the ships could carry were packed in below deck. Once they had left port, they endured a voyage that could take anything from six to ten weeks, depending on weather conditions and the servants' destination.[10] They were provided with only just

---

8   Sacks, David Harris. *The Widening Gate: Bristol and the Atlantic Economy, 1450–1700*. Berkeley: University of California Press, 1991, p.252.

9   Beckles, Hilary MacDonald. *White Servitude and Black Slavery in Barbados, 1627–1715*. Knoxville: University of Tennessee Press, 1989, p.37. From a House of Lords debate of 1647, referring to Barbados.

10 Ibid, p.65.

enough food and drink to meet their basic needs: salt fish or salt beef, stale biscuits, and cheese, and milk and water, which often ran out before the ships stopped at Madeira, the Cape Verde Islands, or the Azores to reprovision.

Outbreaks of disease on board the crowded ships were common, and seasickness was often followed by more serious illnesses such as smallpox, typhoid, and dysentery. Ships' captains expected some deaths, and a loss of 20 per cent of the servant cargo was considered acceptable – but some voyages ended with far greater loss of life.[11]

If Ellin and Jane survived the voyage to St Christopher, they would have landed on an island that was both an English and a French colony. St Christopher had been settled by Sir Thomas Warner in 1623 or 1624 and was the first of England's Leeward Island colonies, but in 1625 the French Captain Pierre Belain d'Esnambuc, while privateering in the area, found refuge on St Christopher after evading an attack by a Spanish ship. He liked what he found, informing his government that the island had great potential for settlement, and as a result of his enthusiastic report France established an interest in taking St Christopher from the English. At the time, Warner needed assistance in fighting both the local Kalinago population and any attempted invasion by Spain – then an enemy of both England and France – so he made an agreement with the French that allowed them to settle alongside the English colonists in return for helping him defend the colony. The combined English and French forces wasted little time in achieving Warner's objective: in 1626 they succeeded in almost wiping out the Kalinago population, and in 1629 successfully repulsed an attack by Spain.

---

11   Ibid, p.66.

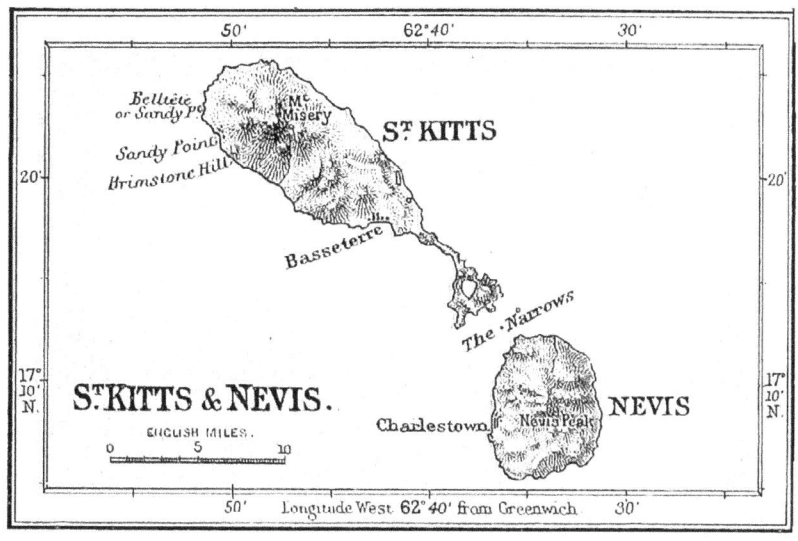

A Map of the Islands of St Christopher and Nevis. From: Lucas, Charles P., A Historical Geography of the British Colonies. Vol 2. Oxford: Clarendon Press, 1888, p.158.

The small plantations on St Christopher's initially grew and traded tobacco, sea island cotton, and indigo,[12] and grew maize, cassava, sweet potatoes, and other tropical vegetables for local consumption. Both tobacco and cotton needed a regular supply of labour to make a profit, so when the indentured servants arrived on the *Robert Bonaventure* the planters were quick to board the ship and compete to buy up the new servants' indentures. These were sold to the highest bidder, and in the early days of St Christopher's colonisation were usually paid for not in money but in pounds of tobacco, which was then an accepted method of payment.[13] When the indentures had all been purchased, the servants disembarked, and Ellin and

---

12 A dark blue dye obtained from the leaves of plants of various members of the genus *Indigofera*, which are native to the tropics.

13 Dyde, Brian. *Out of the Crowded Vagueness: A History of the Islands of St Kitts, Nevis and Anguilla.* Oxford: Macmillan Education, 2005, p.52.

Jane – if they had survived the voyage – may well have had their indentures bought by different planters, and found that they were to be sent to different plantations. Once all the servants had left the ship, the *Robert Bonaventure* loaded up with the profit from the voyage – the goods exchanged for the indentures – and returned to her home port, where the recruiting agents would be paid their share.[14]

The newly landed servants had to come to terms with the strangeness of their new surroundings. The heat and the humidity were exhausting. There were unfamiliar diseases, such as yellow fever and malaria, against which they had no defence. Many of the people they saw looked and sounded unfamiliar, too: the few indigenous Kalinago who had survived the 1626 combined English/French attack and had been allowed to stay on the island; the recently arrived enslaved Africans; and the French planters and their French-speaking servants. The luxuriant tropical flora and fauna were not like anything the new arrivals had been familiar with in Cornwall, and they were certainly unaccustomed to some of the food they were given to eat – the boiled cornmeal, cassava bread, sweet potatoes, plantains, and other local vegetables which they were fed in barely sufficient quantities twice a day, often washed down with a drink made from mashed and fermented sweet potatoes, known as *mobbie*.[15] Salt beef, salt fish, and salt pork was available in small quantities, but fresh meat was reserved for the plantocracy – unless an ox died, when the

---

14 Great Britain. Public Record Office. *Calendar of State Papers, Domestic Series, of the Reign of Charles I: 1631–1633*. London: Longman, Brown, Green, Longmans, and Roberts, 1862, p.251.

15 The word *mobbie* is most likely derived from the Kalinago word for sweet potato: *mabi*. This drink bears little relation to the drink popular today throughout the Caribbean, which is made from the bark of a small tree of the genus *Colubrina*. This is known as *mauby* in the English-speaking Caribbean, *mavi* in the Spanish-speaking Caribbean, and *mabi* in the French-speaking Caribbean.

meat was given to the servants, and the head, tail, feet and entrails to the enslaved Africans.[16] In the early days of colonisation, the newly planted fertile soils enabled the planters to grow sufficient fresh fruit and vegetables to add some variety to the servants' diet, but as sugar became the main crop the planters were so eager to maximise profits from it that they turned over to sugar the land used until then for fruit and vegetables, and the servants' diet became even more limited and unhealthy.

The servants' living accommodations were also unfamiliar and little better – or sometimes even worse – than those they had left behind. They lived in huts similar to those used by the Kalinago, which they had been expected to build for themselves as soon as they arrived at their place of work. In Barbados these were built of sticks bound together with vines, and roofed with plantain leaves. The floor was the bare earth, and the bed and any 'furniture' made of wooden planks.[17] On St Christopher the huts were similarly constructed, although tied together with rope rather than vines and roofed with palm, not plantain, leaves. Guillaume Coppier, an indentured servant in the French part of St Christopher from 1627 to 1630, writes in his *History and Voyage to the West Indies* about the bark of a tree which was used to make the rope for the huts:

> [the Mahaut[18] trees] are located in aquatic areas that are not easily accessible… we strip the tree of its bark and we beat and squeeze it to rid it of all water, then we let it dry in the sun, after

---

16 Beckles, Hilary MacDonald. *White Servitude and Black Slavery in Barbados, 1627–1715.* Knoxville: University of Tennessee Press, 1989, p.96.

17   Beckles, Hilary MacDonald. 'White Labour in Black Slave Plantation Society and Economy: A Case Study of Indentured Labour in Seventeenth Century Barbados,' PhD diss., University of Hull, 1980, p.227.

18 Perhaps he is talking of mangrove here?

which we weave it into rope that we use to secure the structure of our Ajouppas.[19] [20]

He also writes about the palm leaf covering:

We use them to cover the huts. They last for almost two years. When they are dried out by the sun, or when they leak, we replace them with fresh ones… Though the rains are not at all trifling in these areas, we use these leaves here in the same fashion we use slate or bricks [in Lyon, where Coppier was born].[21]

As servants had to make do with such basic housing, where little provision was made for washing and cleaning both themselves and their clothing, it is unsurprising that they were described as 'dirty and unkempt',[22] and it was not until the late 17th century – too late for Ellin and Jane – that legislation was introduced into the English Caribbean colonies to help ensure that indentured servants would be supplied annually with 'the attire necessary for dressing according to the custom of the country'.[23] According to Englishman John Taylor,

---

19   *Ajoupa* or *ajouppa* is the Kalinago word for a hut.
20   Hunt, Gerard M. 'Of the Woods and Trees of these Islands in General.' In *Desperate in Saint Martin: Notes on Guillaume Coppier*. Bloomington: Trafford Publishing, 2013. Kindle edition – unpaginated.
21   Hunt, Gerard M. 'Of their Ajouppas, Cases and Carbeils.' In *Desperate in Saint Martin: Notes on Guillaume Coppier*. Bloomington: Trafford Publishing, 2013. Kindle edition – unpaginated.
22   Beckles, Hilary MacDonald. 'White Labour in Black Slave Plantation Society and Economy: A Case Study of Indentured Labour in Seventeenth Century Barbados.' PhD diss., University of Hull, 1980, p.227.
23   DuPlessis, Robert S. 'Sartorial Sorting in the Colonial Caribbean and North America.' In *The Right to Dress: Sumptuary Laws in a Global Perspective, c.1200–1800*, eds. G. Riello and U. Rublack, pp.346–372. Cambridge: Cambridge University Press, 2019, pp.363–364.

An English Servant Girl, by Wenceslaus Hollar, 1640.

who spent some months in Jamaica in the late 1680s, the clothes provided were barely enough to keep a servant dressed from one year to the next, and he writes that planters gave their indentured servants 'noe more then [sic] the lawes of the island forces 'em to'.[24]

Although the indigenous populations of the islands were mostly seen as 'savages' by the European settlers, when it came to building a shelter, growing fruit and vegetables, or making bread and drink they were quite willing to adopt the well-tried local methods that made good use of available resources and suited the climate of the islands. Coppier devotes a whole chapter of his book to the making of cassava bread, describing the techniques used by the Kalinago women. On the baking of the bread, he writes:

---

24 Ibid., p.364.

A Kalinago Family Outside a Hut, probably in Dominica, by Agostino Brunias, about 1780.

flattened bits of the manioc [cassava] dough must be placed on an iron plate, or on a plate that we make for that purpose from earthenware. [The plate] is placed on a slow clear fire and the manioc [dough] is turned over and over so that this bread, the thickness of a finger, can cook on both sides properly.[25]

Coppier and his companions, and perhaps Ellin and Jane, learnt to make cassava bread for themselves by watching and copying the

---

25 Hunt, Gerard M. 'Of their Bread.' In *Desperate in Saint Martin: Notes on Guillaume Coppier*. Bloomington: Trafford Publishing, 2013. Kindle edition – unpaginated.

Kalinago women, a process that the Cornish women must have found very different from the method they had used to make the barley bread to which they were accustomed.

As they went about their daily tasks, Ellin and Jane would most likely have worked alongside female enslaved Africans, as enslaved workers had arrived on St Christopher as early as 1626, when a group of enslaved men – probably taken from a Spanish ship bound for one of Spain's Caribbean colonies – had been captured and brought to the island. The treatment of servants depended on the individual planter or merchant and was not regulated in any way by the colonial administration until in 1661 Barbados passed *An Act for the Good Governing of Servants, and Ordaining the Rights Between Masters and Servants*. Similar Acts were soon passed by other islands – for example, Jamaica in 1664 and Antigua in 1669 – although in St Christopher the legislation was not adopted until 1722.[26]

To some contemporaries it seemed that servants were treated little better than enslaved men and women, and that they sometimes received even harsher treatment. Richard Ligon, who lived on Barbados between 1647 and 1650, when he seems to have assisted in the management of a plantation, was of this opinion; he writes:

> *The slaves and their posterity, being subject to their Masters for ever, are kept and preserved with greater care than the servants, who are theirs but for five years, according to the law of the Island.*[27] *So that for the time, the servants have the worser lives, for they are put to very hard labor, ill lodging, and their diet very slight.*[28]

---

26 Smith, Robert Emerson. *Colonists in Bondage: White Servitude and Convict Labor in America, 1607–1776*. Chapel Hill: University of North Carolina Press, 1947, p.228.

27 The length of an indenture was sometimes agreed according to the 'custom of the country' – as was the case in Barbados – rather than under English regulations.

28 Ligon, Richard and Karen Ordahl Kupperman. *The True and Exact History of*

The important phrase here is 'for the time', because however harsh the treatment, indentured servants only had to labour for the duration of their indenture, whereas enslaved men and women and their descendants had to labour for life. Servants also had recognised legal rights, including the right to testify and petition in court if they were treated badly. This was a right which servants understood, and courts in the colonies took seriously, with some colonial courts, in accordance with English Common Law, appointing free legal counsel to servants to help ensure they got a fair hearing. In contrast, if the enslaved received harsh treatment they were unable to petition the court, or even to testify as witnesses in court. They had no legally recognised rights.[29]

Throughout their period of indenture women were seen to be of less value than men, and their indentures cost less: in the early days of Caribbean settlement, the price of an indenture for a female servant was about £5, whereas for a male servant it was £6 or £7. And, as Ligon illustrates when he writes of an incident in Barbados where a female indentured servant was to be exchanged for a pig, the owners of servant indentures thought of their servants as nothing more than a commodity:

> *There was a planter in the island who came to his neighbour, and said to him, Neighbour I hear you have lately bought good store of servants, out of the last ship that came from England, and I hear withal, that you want provisions. I have great want of a woman servant; and would be glad to make an exchange. If you will let me have some of your woman's flesh, you shall have some of my hog's flesh; so the price was set at a groat a pound for*

---

the Island of Barbados. Cambridge: Hacket Publishing Company, 2011, p.93. First published in 1657.

29 Suranyi, Anna. *Indentured Servitude: Unfree Labour and Citizenship in the British Colonies*. Montreal: McGill-Queen's University Press, 2021, p.7.

the hog's flesh and six-pence a pound for the Woman's flesh. The scales were set up... but when [the Neighbour] saw how much the Maid outweighed his Sow, he broke off the bargain. Though such a case as this, may seldom happen, yet 'tis an ordinary thing there to sell their servants to one another for the time they have to serve; and in exchange receive any commodities that are in the island.[30]

Female indentured servants had little defence against sexual harassment and rape by their superiors or fellow servants and, as Ann Suranyi notes:

women were often reluctant to report rape because of the difficulty of proof, the possibility of retaliation, and the potential damage to the victim's reputation, factors that still operate as deterrents today.[31]

They were also more likely to be punished for fornication, which was usually revealed by pregnancy; if an indentured servant gave birth while under contract she often received a public whipping, an increase in the length of her indenture – to compensate for the hours of work lost during the pregnancy and birth – and the loss of the child, who could be taken from her and indentured until the age of twenty-one.

Then, if a woman completed her contract, she often received 'freedom dues' of less value than those received by a man – and, moreover – typically of clothing, while men received land, tools, and money or its equivalent in goods such as tobacco. Once a woman was freed from

---

30 Ligon, Richard and Karen Ordahl Kupperman. *The True and Exact History of the Island of Barbados*. Cambridge: Hacket Publishing Company, 2011, p.112. First published in 1657.

31 Suranyi, Anna. *Indentured Servitude: Unfree Labour and Citizenship in the British Colonies*. Montreal: McGill-Queen's University Press, 2021, p.142.

her indenture she had limited options as she sought to make her way in the world. In the early days of settlement, marriageable women were in short supply, and she could then have married, or become the kept mistress of a planter or merchant[32] but as colonial society became more established and Ladies of Quality began to arrive in the Caribbean islands as part of the planter's family, female indentured servants were no longer in such demand as potential wives. It was, however, important for a freed female to marry; those who remain unmarried were likely to be seen as 'masterless women' who would behave in a disorderly manner and encourage men to lead a life of debauchery.[33] If their behaviour fell below the expectations of the community they could be legally obliged to return to servanthood, the local authorities reserving the right to decide on the amount of their wages.

In spite of these limits on their independence, some freed female servants managed to move on to a life over which they had some agency. Many found work serving in local taverns which often belonged to and were staffed by women like themselves. Here they were employed as cooks, waitresses and – depending on the reputation of the tavern – prostitutes. Cleaning, salting and selling fish was another option, or if they were seamstresses they could find work on a plantation, sewing clothing for servants and enslaved people. They might also be employed as housekeepers in a plantation Great House, where they supervised the female enslaved, or work as nurses in one of the plantation sick houses which looked after ailing servants and enslaved people.[34]

---

32 Suranyi, Anna. 'Willing to Go if They Had Their Clothes: Early Modern Women and Indentured Servitude.' In *Challenging Orthodoxies: The Social and Cultural Worlds of Early Modern Women; Essays Presented to Hilda L. Smith*, eds. Sigrun Haude and Melinda S. Zook, pp.193–210. Abingdon: Routledge, 2016, p.205.

33 Ibid, p.194.

34 Ibid, p.144.

We do not know whether Ellin and Jane survived the voyage to St Christopher and completed their term of indenture or, if so, whether they lived to receive their freedom dues and become part of the local community – or if, like many, they died from disease, lack of adequate food and drink, overwork, or excessive punishment before their contract was completed.

As agricultural development in the English Caribbean colonies changed focus from its reliance on small plantations growing a variety of crops to large enterprises capable of producing sugar, and plantations grew in complexity, the demand for indentured servants continued; but as the general agricultural labourers and domestics were replaced by enslaved Africans, the indentured servants were increasingly expected to possess specific skills. For women these included the ability to make clothing for the labour force and the planters and their families, and for men skill in building houses and plantation buildings, and in making the barrels in which the sugar was packed and shipped.

Cornish women were still among the indentured servants who came to the Caribbean, usually leaving from ports such as Plymouth or Bristol. One Cornish woman who left from Bristol in 1660 was Elinor Rodin. We know something of her background and her indenture contract from the Bristol Register, which had been established in 1654 to try and combat the Spirits, who continued to kidnap men and women to fill the need for labour in distant colonies. The Bristol Register records that Elinor was a spinster from Falmouth,[35] a harbour town on the south coast of Cornwall, founded in 1613 by Sir John Killigrew on land surrounding his home,

---

35 Virtual Jamestown. Registers of Servants Sent to Foreign Plantations. Bristol Registers 1654–1686. Elinor Rodin. Accessed 29 August 2021, http://www.virtualjamestown.org/indentures/search_indentures.cgi?search_type=individ&id=2083&db=bristol_ind

Arwenack Manor House, and in its early stages of development when she left for Bristol. Elinor was indentured on 13 November 1660, for four years. Her agent – the person who had organised her indenture and to whom she was bound until her indenture was sold – was one George Vincent.[36]

Elinor was to be shipped to Nevis,[37] the small island close to St Christopher which, on the initiative of Sir Thomas Warner, had been settled by a group of men and women – many of whom were servants who had completed their term of indenture – in 1628.[38] Elinor's arrival in Nevis in 1660 coincided with the rapid development of the sugar industry on the island. Growing numbers of indentured servants were needed if the sugar plantations were to function efficiently, and between 1660 and 1669 there were 811 indentured servants who left the port of Bristol for Nevis, a huge increase over the 43 who had made the journey during the previous decade.[39] We don't know how Elinor was employed on Nevis, but her indenture was most likely tied in some way to the booming sugar industry. As with Ellin Nancarro and Jane Trewin, we have no information about Elinor after she had boarded the ship for Nevis. Did she survive the voyage and complete the four years of her indenture? Did she receive her freedom dues, marry and settle in Nevis? Or did she even leave the island for a more recently established colony, such as Jamaica, which offered new opportunities?

Jamaica was taken from Spain by the English in 1655 as part of Oliver Cromwell's ambitious plan to acquire new colonies in the

---

36   Ibid.
37   Ibid.
38   Columbus named the cloud-topped island *Nuestra Señora de las Nieves – Our Lady of the Snows*. Nevis, pronounced 'Neevis', is the Anglicised corruption of Nieves.
39   Watts, David. *The West Indies: Patterns of Development, Culture and Environmental Change since 1492*. Cambridge: Cambridge University Press, 1987, p.361.

Americas,[40] and as the island had plenty of agricultural land available, grants were offered to encourage settlers to come and develop its potential. Settlers from the early English colonies of Barbados and the Leeward Islands, where land was no longer easily available – and where the owners of small plantations growing a mixture of cash crops found themselves unable to put together the resources needed to make the transition to sugar production – were eager to move to Jamaica and take advantage of the land grants on offer. These 'regional colonists' often went as a family unit, bringing their servants with them, and perhaps Elinor would have been one of their number.[41]

The early period of agricultural development in colonial Jamaica saw the establishment of small to medium sized holdings, of between 50 and 600 acres, which needed a modest capital outlay of no more than £500. As well as sugar, a variety of crops were grown on them, including cocoa, timber, indigo, tobacco, cotton, and ginger, and the labour force comprised small numbers of both enslaved Africans and indentured servants who, while they were being replaced by enslaved workers in the Leeward Islands and Barbados, continued to be a major part of plantation life in Jamaica.[42]

One servant who went to Jamaica from England in 1685 was Cornishwoman Elizabeth Ayres.[43] Although many Cornish servants left from the ports of Plymouth and Bristol, which were relatively near to home, some, including Elizabeth – perhaps

---

40 The Western Design called for the invasion of Hispaniola, but after this part of the plan had failed it was poorly defended Jamaica that became the target and was successfully taken.
41 Mair, Lucille Mathurin. *A Historical Study of Women in Jamaica: 1655–1844*. Kingston: University of the West Indies Press, 2006, p.23.
42 Ibid, p.26.
43 Virtual Jamestown. Registers of Servants Sent to Foreign Plantations. London Registers 1682–1692. Elizabeth Ayres. http://www.virtualjamestown.org/indentures/search_indentures.cgi?search_type=individ&id=38&db=london1_ind

having already left home in search of employment – travelled from ports further afield. Her family was from the ancient market town of Launceston, which in Elizabeth's time was the county town of Cornwall and the site of the County Assizes, but Elizabeth left from the port of London. With the 'consent of Elizabeth Volereen, her aunt',[44] she was indentured for four years on 31 March 1685, one of six women sent to Jamaica during that year by the agent Joseph Bartholomew,[45] and one of a total of forty-six female and ninety-eight male indentured servants sent to Jamaica that year.[46] The occupations of Elizabeth's group of women are not listed, but the individuals who survived the voyage were probably destined to serve in a domestic capacity. As in the case of Ellin and Jane on St Christopher, and Elinor on Nevis, we don't know if Elizabeth survived the voyage or completed her four years of indenture in Jamaica and received her freedom dues.

These four cornish women are shadowy figures. If they had not been kidnapped by the Spirits they may have made the choice to become indentured in an effort to improve their lives, but with few alternative paths available to them there was little opportunity for them to choose differently, and once they had been indentured their lives were controlled by others. Initially, control was in the hands of the recruiting agents and although some of the emigrants

---

44 Ibid.
45 Virtual Jamestown. Registers of Servants Sent to Foreign Plantations. London Registers 1682–1692. Agent Joseph Bartholomew. Accessed 30 August 2021, http://www.virtualjamestown.org/indentures/search_indentures.cgi?search_type=basic&start_page=0&db=london1_ind&servant_ln=&servant_fn=&servant_place=&servant_occ=&destination=&ship=&year-ops=&year=&year1=&agent_ln=Bartholomew&agent_fn=Joseph&agent_place=&agent_occ=&result_order=&submit=Initiate+Search
46 Beckles, Hilary MacDonald. *White Servitude and Black Slavery in Barbados, 1627–1715*. Knoxville: University of Tennessee Press, 1989, p.45.

knew enough about the system to be able to bargain with the agents concerning both their destination and the length of their indenture, it was usually the agent who drew up the details of the indenture, with little input from the servant. Once the servants reached their destination and their indenture was bought, their lives were controlled by the purchaser of that indenture and, despite the introduction of legislation to regulate the management of servants, they had little control over the terms of their service. If they disobeyed the regulations their indenture could be lengthened. At the whim of the owner of their indenture the contract could be resold, used to pay a debt, or gambled away. The servants could not marry without the permission of the owner of their indenture. As women, if they completed their contract they received less valuable freedom dues than their male counterparts, and once freed were limited in the employment options that existed. They may have set sail for the Caribbean in hope of making a better life for themselves, but they would have found too late that the life of an indentured female servant – overworked, ill-fed and badly clothed – was often both unpleasant and short.

As the 18th century progressed and enslaved African women increasingly replaced female indentured servants throughout the Caribbean, few indentured women came to the region. But after the 1834 emancipation of enslaved people in the British Caribbean, and the end of the apprenticeship system in 1838 (which had bound slaves to their plantations for a further term) there was, as at the beginning of European colonisation, a shortage of cheap agricultural labour. To meet the demand for labour the European powers again resorted to the indenture system, but this time they drew their workers from overseas. In the case of Britain's Caribbean colonies, many of the labourers came from India, at the time a part of the

British Empire, and from China, where British economic influence was strong. Indentured servitude would continue in the Caribbean until the early part of the 20th century.

2

Ladies of Quality

The widow Margery Price (1704–1765) was fifty-four years old when in 1758 she left her comfortable family home in Penzance for Jamaica. Twenty-two years earlier she had married John Price (1712–1739), a wealthy member of the Price family who owned a number of substantial sugar plantations in Jamaica. John had been born in Jamaica, but had come to England as a young man to further his education, along with his elder brothers Charles (1708–1772) and Thomas Rose (1711–1731). The English climate did not, however, suit John, whose health was never robust, and he unfortunately soon became ill with the early signs of pulmonary tuberculosis. Searching for a means to help John recover from his illness, his brother Charles – then at Trinity College, Oxford – sought the advice of his tutor, the well-respected physician, Cornishman Dr Frank Nicholls. The doctor had been born at Trereife House, near the town of Penzance, and he recommended the mild climate and sea breeze of that town as a cure, arranging for John to stay with Margery's family, the Badcocks. They were a reasonably well-to-do Cornish family who lived on Chapel Street in the most fashionable part of town; Margery's father, Henry Badcock, had at one time been Collector of Customs for Penzance, and her mother, Parthesia Keigwin, was related to the wealthy Godolphin family. Romance bloomed between Margery and John, and after their marriage in 1736, John built a substantial house at the top of Chapel Street, where their son John (1738–1797) was born. A year later John Senior left Penzance for Jamaica, where his brother Charles was struggling to manage the family estates alone, following the death of Thomas Rose in 1731. But John was unable to adjust to the humid tropical climate, and after spending only a few months in Jamaica he died in early 1739, leaving Margery to bring up their son.[47]

By 1758 John Junior was twenty years of age, ready to familiarise himself with the property he had inherited on his father's death and to assist his Uncle Charles in running the family estates. His mother accompanied him, perhaps to offer support to her only child as he came to terms with the hands-on business of running a sugar estate, but more importantly because her husband, who must have had confidence in her administrative capability, had made her sole executrix of his will, which he had written in September 1738 before leaving Penzance for Jamaica.[48] This gave her the responsibility of administering his considerable estate and executing the provisions of his will, which she could do more effectively from Jamaica.

How would this middle-aged, upper middle-class woman from Penzance fare as a member of Jamaican planter society? She knew she had married into one of the most prominent families among the wealthy Jamaican plantocracy, but she may well have been overawed by the size and grandeur of the Price family's properties, which included Lluidas House, a grand residence in Spanish Town – then the capital of the colony – Worthy Park Estate in Lluidas Vale, in St

---

47 Sparrow, Elizabeth. *The Prices of Penzance: The Influence of 18th Century Jamaican Sugar Plantation Owners on West Cornwall*. Penzance: Sparrow, 1984, pp.2–3.
48 *John Price of Penzance, the Elder: Profile & Legacies Summary 1712–1740*. Accessed 1 October 2021, https://www.ucl.ac.uk/lbs/person/view/2146640647

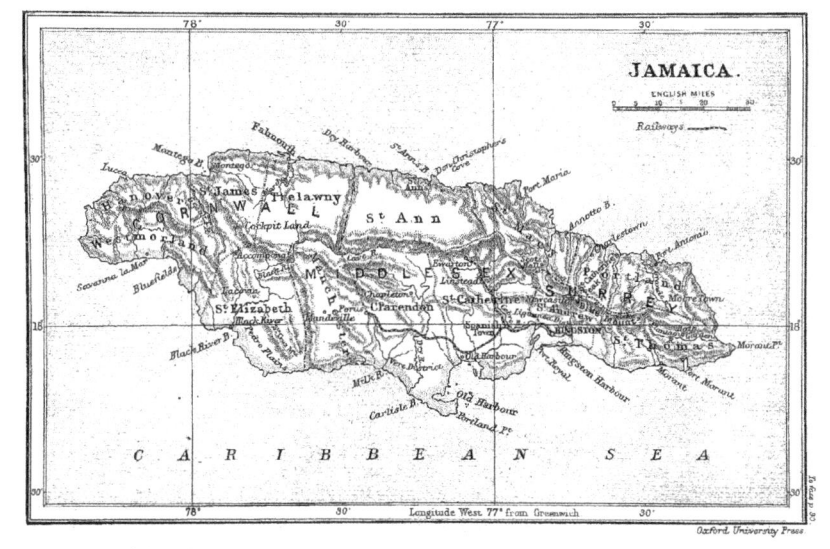

A Map of the Island of Jamaica. From: Lucas, C. P. Historical Geography of the British Colonies. Vol 2. Oxford: Clarendon Press, 1888, p.113.

John's Parish,[49] Rose Hall Estate in St Thomas-in-the-Vale,[50] and the Decoy Estate up in the hills in St Mary.

As Margery set about administering her husband's estates she may well have found that she had little in common with the female members of Jamaica's plantocracy. Colonial Ladies of Quality were generally seen as incapable of playing a part in the business management of the sugar estates where they lived. As they were expected to be docile and pure in thought and deed, their activities were usually limited to the domestic sphere: producing children – preferably male – to ensure the continuation of the family line, and managing the estate's Great House and the mostly female enslaved

---

49 The Parish of St John became part of the Parish of St Catherine in 1866.
50 The Parish of St Thomas-in-the-Vale also became part of the Parish of St Catherine in 1866.

people who worked within it.[51] These 'Ladies' often mistreated the enslaved women they managed, yet strove at all times to make it appear that all was running smoothly. As Maria Nugent, the wife of George Nugent, Jamaica's governor from 1801 to 1805, writes – while euphemistically referring to enslaved people as 'servants':

> *As for the ladies, they appear to me perfect viragos; they never speak but in the most imperious manner to their servants, and are constantly finding fault. West India houses are so thin, that one hears every word, and it is laughable, in the midst of the clamour, to walk out of my room, and see nothing but smiles and good humour.*[52]

Margery was now mistress of the Great House at Worthy Park and, willing or not, she was expected to socialise according to her position in society: to be on friendly terms with the wives of other wealthy sugar planters, to feel superior to the mistresses of smaller properties, and to not mix at all with women from the lower classes. For entertainment, this élite group of women organised and attended dances, dinner parties, and teas; joined literary clubs[53] and regularly attended church.[54] Margery was rescued from this limited existence because, far from being a marginalised and passive bystander in the business of running a sugar estate, she was actively involved in the enterprise.

---

51 O'Callaghan, Evelyn. 'Defamiliarizing 'the mistress': Representations of White *Women in the West Indies; Finding the White Woman.'* In *Women Writing the West Indies, 1804–1939: 'A Hot Place, Belonging to Us'*, p.13. London: Routledge, 2004.

52 Nugent, Maria, Lady. *Lady Nugent's Journal: Jamaica One Hundred and Thirty-Eight Years Ago*. Ed. by Frank Cundall. London: West India Committee for the Institute of Jamaica, 1939, p.107.

53 Shepherd, Verene (ed.) *Women in Caribbean History*. Kingston: Ian Randle, 2012, p.27.

54 Ibid., p.24.

Although Margery had been given administrative responsibilities, she had inherited neither property nor enslaved people from her husband, even though as a widow she was legally entitled to own both. Her husband's uncle, Charles, for example, had left his widow Sarah the house in Spanish Town and nine enslaved women, while he had left his unmarried daughter – also named Sarah – the land known as Old Woman's Savanna and eight enslaved women.[55] While a single or widowed woman could be financially independent, once married her ability to own anything in her own right was severely curtailed; under the common law principle of coverture[56] a wife's legal existence was considered to be merged with that of her husband, and she then had no independent legal existence of her own.

While staying at Worthy Park, Margery's son John Junior met Elizabeth Williams Brammer, the daughter of Dr John Brammer, the resident physician at the estate. They married in 1764, and in 1765 Elizabeth gave birth to a son, Charles Godolphin Price. Following the birth of his son, John Junior began to grow tired of living in Jamaica, and to see his future as an absentee planter, while Margery's health was beginning to fail, and she wanted to return to Penzance. The family made plans to leave Jamaica in the middle of 1766, but Margery died in May of that year, which delayed their departure.[57] John and his wife and young son set sail for London – with Margery in her coffin – a little later in the year, arriving in Penzance in September 1766, when Margery was buried in the Price family vault beside her husband, who had also been brought back from Jamaica for burial after his death.[58]

---

55 Craton, Michael and James Walvin. *A Jamaican Plantation: The History of Worthy Park 1670–1970*. Toronto: University of Toronto Press, 1970, p.66.

56 Alternative spelling: *couverture*.

57 Sparrow, Elizabeth. *The Prices of Penzance: The Influence of 18th Century Jamaican Sugar Plantation Owners on West Cornwall*. Penzance: Sparrow, 1984, p.6.

58 Ibid., p.6.

Among the Jamaican sugar planter families who were friends of the Prices were the Longs. Like the Prices, the Longs' settlement on Jamaica predated their connection with Cornwall: the patriarchs of both families, Francis Price (1635–1689) and Samuel Long (1638–1683), had sailed from Britain to the Caribbean as part of Oliver Cromwell's army under the command of General Robert Venables and Admiral William Penn when they took Jamaica from Spain in 1655. Both young men stayed on the island and both received large grants of land, which enabled them to become wealthy and influential landowners.

The Long connection with Cornwall began in the early 1730s with Samuel Long's Jamaica-born grandson, also named Samuel (1700–1757). The younger Samuel aspired to be an absentee planter, and once back in Britain bought a small farm at Tredudwell, near the town of Fowey, which he rebuilt as his country seat and named Tredudwell Manor. While the house was being rebuilt, Samuel leased Roselyon House in St Blazey, near the town of St Austell, living there with his wife, Mary Tate, and their children: Catherine Maria (1727–1812), Robert (1729–1772), and Charles (1731–1776). While at Roselyon, Mary gave birth to three additional children: Susanna Charlotte, known as Charlotte (1733–1818), Edward (1734–1813) and Elizabeth Amelia (1740-1832), sometimes known as Amelia Elizabeth. When Tredudwell Manor was completed in 1741, the Long family moved to their new home and, living on the proceeds of Samuel's Jamaica estates, settled into a peaceful life in rural Cornwall.[59] Their enjoyment of the Cornish countryside proved, however, to be short-lived; poor management of Samuel's Jamaica plantations

---

59 Prykhodko, Yaroslav. 'The Social Life of Edward Long.' In 'Mind, Body, and the Moral Imagination in the Eighteenth-Century British Atlantic World.' PhD diss., University of Pennsylvania, 2011, pp.134, 138. Accessed 8 October 2021, https://repository.upenn.edu/cgi/viewcontent.cgi?article=1719&context=edissertations

threatened his financial stability, so in 1745 he returned to Jamaica with his sons, Robert and Charles, to put his affairs in order.[60]

His youngest son, Edward, was left behind to study at a school in Liskeard, and daughter Elizabeth was sent to a school in London, while Samual instructed his wife Mary, and daughters Catherine and Charlotte, to join him in Jamaica with no delay. Mary, however, had other plans: with the family fortune in peril, she put off sailing from Portsmouth in the hope of arranging profitable marriages for Catherine and Charlotte – who were both of marriageable age – by arranging introductions to suitable gentlemen selected from the numerous naval officers resident in the town. Mary did not seek the advice of her husband for her actions, and here she overstepped the generally accepted boundaries of her domestic responsibilities. Her daughters complained that not only had she acted without Samuel's permission but had not considered their feelings and – worse yet – damaged their reputations as: 'the free admission of many male visitors to the house might have a tendency to injure [their] Characters'.[61] Samuel considered his wife's behaviour to be 'disloyal, imprudent, and lacking in affection to her children, and flew into an outrageous passion'.[62] Mary's marriage did not survive the altercation, and soon after Mary's eventual arrival in Jamaica with her two elder daughters the couple separated. Mary returned to England alone and Samuel forbad her to see her youngest daughter Elizabeth, but Mary – ever resourceful – ignored her husband's orders and arranged with Elizabeth's schoolmistress so that, as her son Edward writes:

---

60   Estate managers were known as attorneys.
61   Prykhodko, Yaroslav. 'The Social Life of Edward Long.' In 'Mind, Body, and the Moral Imagination in the Eighteenth-Century British Atlantic World.' PhD diss., University of Pennsylvania, 2011, p.140. Accessed 8 October 2021, https://repository.upenn.edu/cgi/viewcontent.cgi?article=1719&context=edissertations, p.140.
62   Ibid., p.140.

having placed a high screen in the room where visitors commonly were introduced, a slit was cut in one of the panels, thro' which my mother whenever she came, was indulged with liberty to peep at my Sister, and to hear her sing or play on the Harpsichord.[63]

Mary's ingenuity enabled her to outmanoeuvre her husband's attempts to dictate the life of his family and also enabled Elizabeth to continue her studies. Mary never returned to Jamaica, but despite the marital rift between the couple Samuel left her in his will an annual annuity of £400 secured on his Jamaica estates, and the use of Tredudwell Manor for life.[64] The couple's three daughters went on to make the required advantageous marriages to – as was frequently the case in this sector of society – scions of other wealthy Jamaican planter families.

Catherine married her cousin Henry Moore (1713–1769) in 1751, and the couple had two children: Susanna Jane (1752–1821) and John Henry (1756–1780). Henry Moore had been born in Jamaica to a well-established planter family, and owned land in St Mary's Parish and Vere Parish totalling 1,678 acres.[65] He served as Lieutenant Governor of Jamaica, and Acting Governor on two occasions; first in 1756 and then in 1759–1762, when with ruthless efficiency he put down the uprising of enslaved people known as Tacky's Rebellion, so named because an enslaved man named Tacky had led the first attack in St Mary's Parish, where Moore had property. The rebellion was only suppressed after eighteen months of fighting which left 60 whites dead, over 500 enslaved men and women killed

---

63 Ibid., p.142.
64 *Samuel Long of Tredudwell: Profile & Legacies Summary*. Accessed 12 October 2021, https://www.ucl.ac.uk/lbs/person/view/2146633746
65 Vere Parish was merged into Clarendon Parish in 1866.

Catherine Long. From: Howard, R.M. Records and Letters of the Family of the Longs… London: Simpkin, Marshall, Hamilton, Kent, 1925, p.125.

in battle or executed, and another 500 deported to Nova Scotia in Canada.[66]

As a reward for quelling the rebellion Moore was made a baronet and awarded the Governorship of the Province of New York. Moore's brother-in-law, Edward Long – best remembered for his *History of Jamaica*, which expressed his view that the enslaved, and indeed all Africans, were not only inferior to the white race but barely human – no doubt applauded his brother-in-law's firm actions, but it is unknown what views Henry's wife Catherine held.

It is said that Catherine's Peak, which stands at 4,928 feet (1,502 metres) in St Andrew's Parish, is named after Catherine Long, as she was the first white woman to climb to its summit.[67] [68] Whether true or not, for the story to have some credence she must have been locally perceived as a strong woman capable of making the climb, and from her portrait she appears to be a person of independent character who

---

66 Brunache, Peggy. *Slave Rebellion in the Eighteenth Century: Tacky's Revolt*. Glasgow: University of Glasgow, [2020]. Accessed 15 October 2021, https://www.futurelearn.com/info/courses/slavery-in-the-british-caribbean/0/steps/162134

67 Howard, Robert Mowbray. 'Edward Long's Sisters.' In *Records and Letters of the Family of the Longs of Longville, Jamaica, and Hampton Lodge, Surrey*, p.183. London: Simpkin, Marshall, Hamilton, Kent and Co., 1925.

68 It is also said that the Peak was named after St Catherine.

may, like her mother Mary, have held her own opinions rather than submitting to the views of the male members of her family.

Henry Moore took up his post as Governor of the Province of New York in 1765 and died there in 1769. In his will he gave Catherine the responsibility of acting as his sole executrix, leaving his property in trust for his then 13-year-old son John Henry to a small group of fellow planters, including his brother-in-law, Edward Long. After the early death of John Henry at the age of twenty-six, Catherine and Henry's only remaining child, Susanna, inherited Moore Hall estate, her father's property in St Mary's Parish, Jamaica.[69] Susanna became one of a small number of female owners of substantial sugar estates and numerous enslaved workers, and although when she married she lost control of her inheritance, after her husband's death Moore Hall reverted to her ownership. She left Jamaica for England when she became a widow and, as an absentee planter, employed an attorney to manage her estate. Susanna willed her Jamaican property to her cousin Edward Beeston Long, and when he inherited it after her death in 1821 there were 180 enslaved people at Moore Hall.[70] Her mother Catherine later remarried, becoming the wife of Captain Richard Vincent.[71]

Catherine's younger sister Charlotte also married into the Jamaican sugar plantocracy. Her husband was George Ellis, the owner of Greencastle Estate in St Mary's Parish, a substantial

---

[69] *Moore Hall, Jamaica, St Mary: Estate Details*. Accessed 18 October 2021, https://www.ucl.ac.uk/lbs/estate/view/2526.

[70] *1823 Jamaica Almanac: Return of Givings for the March Quarter, 1822; County of Middlesex, Parish of St. Mary*. Accessed 21 October 2021, http://www.jamaicanfamilysearch.com/Members/a1823_03.htm.

[71] Howard, Robert Mowbray. 'Edward Long's Sisters.' In *Records and Letters of the Family of the Longs of Longville, Jamaica, and Hampton Lodge, Surrey*, p.183. London: Simpkin, Marshall, Hamilton, Kent and Co., 1925.

property which, in 1754, had 536 enslaved workers.[72] George had died in 1753, while Charlotte was pregnant with their first and only child, George. In his will, he had bequeathed his wife £1,200 a year, but unfortunately failed to make any provision for his unborn son. George's younger brother John Ellis saw an opportunity to profit from George's lack of forethought and immediately claimed his brother's inheritance, except for Charlotte's annuity. After difficult negotiations Charlotte was persuaded to allow John Ellis to acquire Green Castle and to surrender £500 of her annuity annually during George Junior's minority. In return John Ellis agreed to pay for the education of the boy, and when he was of age to give him £20,000 and a life interest in another of the Ellis family properties, the Caymanas sugar plantation.[73] With no experience in working through the complicated laws as they related to family inheritance, Charlotte was taken advantage of, and both she and George lost considerable financial capital because of this agreement.

The widowed Charlotte and her son soon left Jamaica for England, arriving at Gravesend, where they were met by Charlotte's sister Catherine, who writes: 'I went to Gravesend to meet my sister Charlotte, then the widow Ellis who with her little boy George, an infant in arms, arrived from Jamaica.'[74]

John Ellis, meanwhile, did not live long to enjoy his 'inheritance' – he was lost at sea in 1782 – but his younger son, Charles Rose Ellis, later made amends for his father's actions. When he came of age in 1792 and inherited his share of the family assets, he gave his cousin

---

72 Hall, Catherine. 'The Slavery Business and the Making of "Race" in Britain and the Caribbean.' *Current Anthropology.* (Vol.61, Supplement 22, October 2020), p.S178.
73 Ibid, p.S178.
74 Gawthorp, Humphrey. 'George Ellis of Ellis Caymanas: A Caribbean Link to Scott and the Bronte Sisters.' *Electronic British Library Journal* (2005), p.3 Accessed 22 October 2021, https://www.bl.uk/eblj/2005articles/article3.htmlf

George £10,000 in cash as part-reparation for the inheritance he had lost.[75]

Charlotte soon remarried, becoming the wife of Sir David Lindsay of Evelick, and she bore him six children, one of whom, William, continued the family's Caribbean connection: he owned Orange Hill Estate on Tobago and in 1794 became governor of the island.[76] After the death of her second husband in 1797, Charlotte took a small house at Sunning Hill[77] in Berkshire, where her daughter Elizabeth kept her company. It overlooked Bagshot Heath, giving Charlotte a view which she compared unfavourably with the Jamaican landscape, describing it as that 'dreary prospect of Bagshot Heath, uncommonly barren and extensive'.[78] She died at her house in Sunning Hill in 1818.

The youngest of the three Long sisters, Elizabeth, continued to live in London after she completed her schooling, and in 1763 married the Jamaican planter Samuel Heming[79] (1714–1773). On the death of his father in 1755, Samuel had inherited Seville Plantation in the Parish of St Ann, a substantial property. Like the Longs, the Heming family patriarch, Captain Samuel Hemmings, had gone to Jamaica with Penn and Venables in 1655 and settled there, acquiring a land grant of 2,500 acres which included Sevilla la Nueva, a settlement established on the site of a Taino village by the Spanish in 1509 as the first capital of Jamaica. Captain Hemmings had named his estate New Seville and began to develop a successful

---

75 Ibid., p.5.
76 Woodcock, Henry Iles. *A History of Tobago*. Ayr: Smith and Grant, 1867, p.230.
77 Now spelt Sunninghill.
78 Howard, Robert Mowbray. 'Edward Long's Sisters.' In *Records and Letters of the Family of the Longs of Longville, Jamaica, and Hampton Lodge, Surrey*, p.194. London: Simpkin, Marshall, Hamilton, Kent and Co., 1925.
79 The surname was originally spelt Hemings or Hemmings but was later spelt Heming.

sugar plantation there, building a two-storey Great House in the 1670s.[80]

Samuel and Elizabeth Hemings sailed for Jamaica soon after their marriage and moved into the Great House, recently rebuilt as a single-storey dwelling after a hurricane had removed almost the entire top storey of the original house.[81] Here Elizabeth would give birth to six children, but her husband did not live long to enjoy his family; he died in 1773, leaving his wife again pregnant, and with his business affairs in disarray. He made a will shortly before he died, leaving his property in the hands of a small group of fellow planters, including his brother-in-law Edward Long and Charles Price, and giving them the responsibility for making provision for his wife, young children and unborn child.[82] He did not see fit to make his widow an executrix to his will, so she played no part in the administration of the Heming property.

Elizabeth returned to England and moved into a house in Chichester, Sussex, where she lived with continual anxieties about her financial stability. Her sister Charlotte, now Lady Lindsay, wrote to her brother Edward about Elizabeth's straitened circumstances in November 1786:

> *Poor Mrs Hemming's Fate has been a very melancholy one, tho' even she has cause to be thankful that Providence has given her such a friend as she has met with in you: otherwise what would become of her and her children.*[83]

---

80 Seville Heritage Park. Accessed 25 October 2021, https://whc.unesco.org/en/tentativelists/5431.

81 Ibid.

82 *Samuel Heming of St Catherine: Profile & Legacies Summary*, ????–1773. Accessed 25 October 2021, https://www.ucl.ac.uk/lbs/person/view/2146648853

83 Howard, Robert Mowbray. 'Edward Long's Sisters.' In *Records and Letters of the Family of the Longs of Longville, Jamaica, and Hampton Lodge, Surrey*, p.249. London: Simpkin, Marshall, Hamilton, Kent and Co., 1925.

The following year Elizabeth wrote to Edward, asking for his help in paying her bills, including the school fees of her son, Beeston Henry, the child born after her husband's death:

> *I'm necessitated to trouble you on the old and to me disagreeable subject money, the emptiness of a longer delay. Mr. Cole having wrote me yesterday his school has already begun and that he expected Beeston's return daily, inclosing his account likewise, the amount of which I wish to send with B. …I have not a farthing left to pay Mr Cole or buy Beeston a new suit of Cloaths, nor even to keep house, take compassion on me therefore my Dr Brother, for without your assistance, what can I do.*[84]

In this letter Elizabeth uses the subservient words of a dependent Lady of Quality, apologising for her situation, but with the profits from her deceased husband's properties still tied up in the complicated arrangements of his will, she perhaps rarely received an annuity from the estate's trustees, so would have had little to live on. Nevertheless, despite her straitened financial circumstances, she lived to the age of ninety-two and on her death in 1832, after spending much of her life in Chichester, she was buried in Chichester Cathedral. Like his cousin William, her son Beeston kept up the family links to the Caribbean, spending much of his life on the island of Grenada.[85]

All three of the Long sisters returned to England when they were widowed, although none returned to Cornwall, preferring, like many members of the planter class, to settle in London or the home counties, where they could more easily influence the policy of the British government in the West Indian Interest, enjoy the delights

---

84   Ibid., p.251.
85   Ibid., p.195.

of a sophisticated social life, and mix with other absentee planter families.

Five years after Catherine Long's first husband, Sir Henry Moore, completed his term of duty as Acting Governor of Jamaica, Cornishman William Trelawny (1722–1772) was appointed the island's governor. He was the second member of the family to hold the post, his cousin Edward Trelawny (1699–1754) having served as governor from 1738 until ill health caused him to retire in 1751. The Trelawnys frequently married within the family: William was the son of Royal Navy Captain William Trelawny and his wife, Mary Bisset of Trelawne Manor, which lies in Pelynt, near Looe on the south coast of Cornwall; and William Junior married his cousin, Laetitia Trelawny, the daughter of his uncle, Sir Harry Trelawny, and his wife Laetitia Trelawny – who were also cousins. Sir Harry's branch of the family lived at Budshead Manor in the Parish of St Budeaux, which lies on the east bank of the Tamar River just into Devon.[86]

The Trelawnys were well-established and influential members of the Cornish gentry whose political power largely derived from their control of the rotten boroughs[87] of East and West Looe. Several members of the family served as Members of Parliament for both constituencies, and the Trelawnys were therefore well positioned to influence the appointment of one of their own to a lucrative colonial position such as Governor of Jamaica, a post which carried 'handsome emoluments, estimated at between £8,500 and £10,000

---

86 Laetitia and Anne were therefore born in Devon, not Cornwall, but given the Cornish heritage of the Trelawny family and the intermarriage between the Cornish and Devon branches of the family, they have been included in this chapter.

87 A rotten borough was a community which had decreased so much in size and population that it no longer justified separate parliamentary representation but was nevertheless still entitled to elect and send one or more Members of Parliament. West Looe by the 18th century had a population of about 1,000 but was entitled to two Members of Parliament until the Reform Act of 1845.

yearly, with attractive prospects of added trading fees and prizes for seized vessels.'[88]

Laetitia accompanied her husband William to Jamaica, leaving her two children in the care of her family and arriving in 1768, along with her twin sister Anne (1728–1772) and Cornishman Dr John Walcott (1738–1819), the governor's personal physician. The new governor and his family moved into the palatial King's House, the governor's residence in Spanish Town, which had been recently rebuilt and refurbished at considerable expense. The governor was the King's representative – the nearest thing to Royalty on the island – and Laetitia and Anne, although they had grown up in a well-to-do family, were most likely unprepared for life at the pinnacle of colonial Jamaica's society.

The arrival of a new governor and his wife and family was an event which aroused much curiosity around the island, and Laetitia and Anne would have had to accept that they would be closely scrutinised by both the élite members of society and the general public. Another governor's wife, Maria Nugent, after attending her first formal meal at King's House which – as it was paid for out of the public purse in order to welcome to the new governor and his wife – was open for all to observe, experienced considerable discomfort at being the focus of so much attention. She writes:

> *All the population I believe, both white and black, were admitted to walk round the table and stare at me after dinner… being, I suppose, very curious to see what sort of looking people we were; but their curiosity added exceedingly to the heat and, indeed, I never felt anything like it in all my life.*[89]

---

[88] Mair, Lucille Mathurin. *A Historical Study of Women in Jamaica: 1655–1844.* Kingston: University of the West Indies Press, 2006, p.101.

[89] Nugent, Maria, Lady. *Lady Nugent's Journal: Jamaica One Hundred and Thirty-Eight Years Ago.* Ed. Frank Cundall. London: West India Committee for the Institute of

King's House in Spanish Town, Jamaica, in the 1840s. From: Duperly, Adolpe. Daguerian Excursions in Jamaica. Kingston: Jamaica [1844?].

The tropical heat took some getting used to, especially during the numerous crowded and lively balls and other festivities which regularly took place in Spanish Town, most frequently between October and December – mercifully, the cooler months of the year – when the Assembly met to represent and put forward to the governor the local interests of the colony. As the governor's wife, Laetitia would be expected to dress regally when attending the festivities and to possess the stamina needed to dance for long hours with the local and visiting gentlemen who always outnumbered any available female dancing partners. As Maria Nugent writes after attending a ball given in her honour by the Council:

> [*I put on*] *my smartest dress, with a gold tiara and white feathers*

Jamaica, 1939, p.20.

and made myself look as magnificent as I could… Danced myself almost to death, to please both civil and military, Army and Navy, and stayed till 1 o'clock.[90]

Laetitia was expected to support her husband not only by participating in social activities but by being at his side during all his various – sometimes tedious – ceremonial activities such as troop inspections, and accompanying William on the official visits he made to all parts of the island, no matter how remote or inaccessible. It was important for her to be on affable terms with the local planters who hosted the governor and his wife during these visits, and whose interests were often at odds with the government policy which the governor was responsible for implementing. Socially she was expected to provide tactful support to her husband by being on casually friendly terms with the élite, but was not encouraged to develop any special friendships which might inflame the jealousies which flared up between local families as they competed for the governor's attention. As the Trelawnys were not of the local plantocracy it was perhaps not too difficult to avoid these complications, and Laetitia at least had her sister Anne to whom she could turn for support.

Unfortunately, neither Laetitia nor Anne seems to have left any correspondence from their time in Jamaica, so we have little idea if, as was expected of them, they were comfortable in supporting the governor and his policies, or if they had any wish or opportunity to act independently outside of their limited support role. We also know little of them as individual characters, although Dr Walcott describes Anne as a woman 'who had many natural good qualities.'[91]

---

90 Ibid., p.57.
91 Redding, Cyrus. *Fifty Years' Reflections, Literary and Personal, with Observations on*

He also apparently found her very credulous, and to prove his point tells the following anecdote:

> [O]n her asking the news one morning, [I] told her that a cherub had been caught up in the Blue Mountains, and brought into the town.
> 'What did they do with it, my dear doctor?'
> 'Put it in a cage with a parrot.'
> 'And what then, doctor?'
> 'In the morning the parrot had pecked out both its eyes.'
> 'You don't say so!' [92]

He seems to have dismissed the possibility that she was being sarcastic rather than credulous in her response!

Throughout the Trelawnys' time in Jamaica, the danger of death from malaria or yellow fever would never have been far from their thoughts, as the death of colleagues and acquaintances was an ongoing and regular occurrence. As Maria Nugent writes, 'of late I have omitted to mention illness, for it only makes one melancholy and miserable; but there are in fact, only three topics of conversation here, – debt, disease and death. It is, indeed, truly shocking.'[93] Death would catch up with the Trelawnys in 1772. Anne died of yellow fever in the earlier part of the year and was buried 'under ye Governor's seat in ye Church at Spanish Town.'[94] After Anne's death Dr Walcott was

---

Men and Things. Vol.1. London: Charles J. Skeete, 1858, p.266. Accessed 3 November 2021, https://lordbyron.org/monograph.php?doc=CyReddi.1858&select=ContentsI

92 Ibid., pp.265–266.

93 Nugent, Maria, Lady. *Lady Nugent's Journal: Jamaica One Hundred and Thirty-Eight Years Ago*. Ed. Frank Cundall. London: West India Committee for the Institute of Jamaica, 1939, p.239.

94 William Trelawny – Burial – From the St Budeaux Parish Church Records. National Library of Jamaica News Clipping File.

moved to write an elegy, 'The Nymphis of Tauris', in her honour. His poem was included in a work entitled *Persian Love Elegies*, which was published in Kingston by Joseph Thompson and Co. in 1773. It was the first book of poetry to be published in Jamaica.[95]

Governor William died of yellow fever in December of the same year. He had been a popular governor with both the Assembly and the Council, and in recognition of his service the colony voted to bear the expenses of his funeral and burial.[96] Laetitia, devastated by the deaths of both her sister and husband in such a short period of time, returned to England, accompanied by Dr Walcott. It is said that 'a serious attachment took place'[97] between herself and the doctor on the journey home and a marriage was supposedly planned, but before any such union could take place, Laetitia died, in May 1775, and Dr Walcott returned to Truro, where he went back to practising medicine.

In Truro Walcott socialised with the great and the good of the town, including members of the Daniell family, wealthy mine owners and merchants whose patriarch, Thomas Daniell (1720–1810), had been known as 'Guinea-a-Minute Daniell' because of his money-making skills.[98] To show off his wealth Thomas had built the Mansion House on Princes Street in Truro, a palatial residence which on his death had been inherited by his only son, Ralph Allen Daniell (1762–1823).

---

95 Cundall, Frank. 'The Press and Printers of Jamaica Prior to 1820.' *Proceedings of the American Antiquarian Society*, p.303. (Vol.26, October 1916). Accessed 3 November 2021, https://www.americanantiquarian.org/proceedings/44806619.pdf.

96 Ibid.

97 Redding, Cyrus. *Fifty Years' Reflections, Literary and Personal, with Observations on Men and Things*. Vol.1. London: Charles J. Skeete, 1858, p.265. Accessed 3 November 2021, https://lordbyron.org/monograph.php?doc=CyReddi.1858&select=ContentsI

98 Walcott was an early patron of the Cornish painter John Opie (1761–1807) who painted Thomas Daniell in 1786.

The Mansion House with a View of Prince's Street, Truro, by T. Wheatley. The house is on the far left of the painting and still stands. Image made available through the Paul Mellon Centre for Studies in British Art, from the website Art and the Country House. Accessed 15 November 2021, https://artandthecountryhouse.com/catalogues/catalogues-index/the-mansion-house-with-a-view-of-princes-street-truro-1034

A successful businessman like his father, Ralph Allen Daniell married Elizabeth Mason Pooley, the wealthy heiress and niece of Ralph Allen, who had moved from Cornwall to Bath, Somerset, in his youth and made his fortune by investing in stone quarries that produced the distinctive Bath stone used in the development of Georgian Bath.

Ralph Allen Daniell became Member of Parliament for East Looe, and was Sheriff of Cornwall from 1795 to 1796, but although he was wealthy the local gentry did not consider him to be a member of their élite group; one of their number once referred to his wife Elizabeth as being married to 'a common coal merchant' because his business interests included supplying coal to the local mines.[99] Eager to rise in local society and aware that ownership of a luxurious town house was not enough, Ralph purchased Trelissick, a large country estate in the Parish of Feock, near Truro. The house is set in extensive grounds overlooking the River Fal; Ralph expanded and developed the estate, creating rides through the surrounding woods and buying up any available surrounding land.[100] [101]

Ralph's wife Elizabeth gave birth to sixteen children, of whom thirteen survived to adulthood: some were born at the Mansion House, others at Trelissick. Elizabeth's thirteenth child, daughter Anne, was born in 1801 and, like her siblings, as a young woman had the opportunity to visit her wealthy Allen family relations in Bath. It is in Bath that she probably met Jamaican-born Lieutenant Hinton East (1783–1866), whom she married at the church of Bathwick St Mary's, near Bath, in 1824.

Hinton East was a member of a family which, like the Prices, the Longs, and the Hemings, had settled in Jamaica during the early days of British colonisation. Hinton's great-grandfather, Captain John East, having arrived with the invading forces of Penn and Venables in 1655, had decided to stay, acquired considerable land grants, and established the East family as wealthy and influential planters.

Anne accompanied her husband out to Jamaica in the early 1830s and, with their children Mary Elizabeth (1825–1894), Edward Hinton (1826–1862), Isabella Anne (1828–1905), and Janetta Gertrude (1833–1884), moved into Raymond Hall, the Great

---

[99] 'Cornish Families: The Daniells.' In *One and All: A Cornish Monthly Illustrated Journal* (March 1869) p.11.

[100] Blake, Colin and Feock Parish Council. *Feock Trails – History Information: Historic Houses – Trelissick.* Accessed 15 November 2021, https://www.feockpc.com/trelissick

[101] Trelissick is now a National Trust property and is open to the public.

Trelissick House by Thomas Hosmer Shepherd (1793–1864).
From the author's collection.

House of Maryland coffee estate which lies up in the Blue Mountains and, along with the neighbouring Creighton coffee estate,[102] belonged to Hinton's half-brother, Sir Edward Hyde East (1764–1847).[103] Sir Edward – judge, legal writer, one-time Chief Justice of the Supreme Court in India, Member of Parliament and member of the Privy Council – was an absentee planter who owned several sugar plantations in addition to his coffee estate holdings. Hinton, as Planting Attorney, was to manage the Blue Mountains coffee estates on Sir Edward's behalf. The position of plantation manager was

---

102 Creighton still produces coffee. Now called Craigton Blue Mountain Coffee Estate, the company provides tours of the Estate and Great House.
103 Hinton East's father married twice: Sir Edward Hyde East was his son by his first marriage, to Amy Hall, and Captain Hinton East his son by his second wife, Mary Wilkins.

seen as a Middling Sort of occupation by élite colonial society, but as Hinton was a member of a well-established family who owned large sugar plantations he and his wife were considered to be part of Jamaica's plantocracy.

Anne and Hinton arrived during an unstable period in Jamaica's history. From the early 17th century, as the number of black enslaved people in the Caribbean increased in relation to the small number of white plantation owners, the owners grew fearful of uprisings among the enslaved workers. In Jamaica these fears were realised when in 1831 Jamaica experienced one of the largest rebellions of enslaved people in the British Caribbean: the Sam Sharpe Rebellion, named after the enslaved, native-born Baptist deacon who was one of its leaders. The rebellion was put down with the full force available to the colonial administration, which then executed over 300 hundred enslaved men and women, including Sharpe.

In the short term the Sam Sharpe Rebellion failed to bring about better treatment of the enslaved or to cause the British government to consider granting them freedom, but over the next few years several developments caused the British government to move forward with more purpose in its deliberations concerning slavery. Reports of the severe punishment meted out to those who had taken part in the rebellion caused outrage among some in Britain, and in 1823 the government passed resolutions designed to improve the working conditions of the enslaved. These resolutions were largely ignored in the colonies. At the same time, differences were growing within the powerful West Indian lobby between locally based and absentee planters. The former wanted slavery to continue, while the latter were more in favour of emancipation if sufficient financial compensation was provided for the loss of their 'property' – the enslaved. Meanwhile, the price of sugar fell because the plantations were producing too much sugar to meet the Mother Country's needs, and although production was protected by low tariffs which gave the planters access to the British market, the sugar plantations were becoming more of an expense than an asset. The British sugar colonies also faced increased competition from other sources of sugar, such as Cuba and Brazil, where the trade in enslaved people still flourished, helping to keep production costs down.

In 1830, the conservative Tory party government was replaced by the more reform-minded and anti-slavery Whig party, which was able to shepherd through the passage of the Great Reform Act of 1832. This legislation introduced major changes to the electoral system, including the abolition of the rotten boroughs that allowed wealthy supporters of the pro-slavery West Indian Interest to purchase parliamentary seats. A year later the Emancipation Act was passed. It came into effect on 1 August 1834 but gave the enslaved little of the freedom they had anticipated. Only small children under six years old were freed on that date. All other enslaved workers were to be 'apprenticed' for up to eight years. For 75 per cent of their working week, they worked for their former owner. For the remaining 25 per cent they were allowed to work where they chose for a small wage. This period was supposed to 'prepare' the enslaved for their freedom at the end of their 'apprenticeship', and was adopted by all the British Caribbean colonies except for Antigua and Barbuda, where the slave owners, determining that it was cheaper for them to pay a daily wage than to feed and house their formerly enslaved workers, freed them on the day the Emancipation Act came into force.

In 1835 the British government approved the provision of financial compensation to former owners of enslaved workers. Approximately £20 million was paid out, with Sir Edward Hyde East receiving compensation of £4,043 16s 5d for the 214 enslaved people he had owned on Maryland Estate,[104] just one of his several estates. The previously enslaved received nothing.

Working conditions for the 'apprentices' changed little from those they had endured as enslaved people, and as discontent grew among those who sought to end slavery a campaign to bring an end to the apprenticeship period began. The campaign succeeded, and the British Parliament at last voted for complete emancipation, which came into effect on 1 August 1838. In theory, the freed men and women could now work where they chose, and on some islands there were abandoned plantations and waste land available for cultivation where they could work their own land and establish villages; the aptly named Liberta in St Paul's Parish, Antigua, and Time and Patience in Trelawny Parish, Jamaica, are two examples of these emancipation villages. On other islands, such as Barbados, most agricultural land was already under cultivation, and many of the freed people had to return to the plantations where they had laboured as enslaved people and work in return for low wages.

By the time the Emancipation Act was passed Anne and her family were well settled at Raymond Hall, and here she gave birth to two more children: Emily Matilda (1835–1919) and Francis Hyde (1838–1857). With the death of Sir Edward Hyde East in 1847, the family's social standing among the élite of the island improved, as Anne's husband now became the owner rather than the manager of Maryland Estate and its Great House.

Raymond Hall was well known as a pleasant place to visit and, like Anne's Trelissick home, possessed memorable views over the surrounding landscape. One of Anne's guests was the novelist Anthony Trollope who, after a visit in 1859, wrote in his travel book

---

104 *Maryland – Jamaica – St Andrew*. Accessed 22 November 2021, https://www.ucl.ac.uk/lbs/estate/view/2142

The West Indies and the Spanish Main that 'perhaps the finest view in the island is from Raymond Lodge [*sic*], a house high up among the mountains'.[105] Trollope enjoyed spending time with the wealthy planters but he had negative views of Jamaica's black population, writing that although 'capable of the hardest bodily work, and that probably with less bodily pain than men of any other race; …is idle, unambitious as to worldly position, sensual, and content with little. Intellectually, he is apparently capable of but little sustained effort'.[106]

Some years later, in 1887, the author and historian James Anthony Froude visited Anne at Raymond Hall. His views on the black population of the Caribbean, expressed in his book *The English in the West Indies*, echo those of Trollope. After visiting Grenada, he writes:

> *If left entirely to themselves, they would, in a generation or two relapse into savages; there are two alternatives before not Grenada only, but all the English West Indies – either an English administration pure and simple… or a falling eventually into a state like that of Hayti, where they eat the babies, and no white man can own a yard of land.*[107]

Anne's four daughters all married in Jamaica, and even if they did not marry into the highest echelons of colonial society they did make respectable marriages. In 1846 Mary, aged twenty, married the Reverend Colin Maclaverty, an Anglican minister. During her

---

105 Cundall, Frank. *Historic Jamaica; With Fifty-Two Illustrations*. London: West India Committee for the Institute of Jamaica, 1915, p.222–223. Accessed 14 November 2021, https://ia800207.us.archive.org/11/items/cu31924020417527/cu31924020417527.pdf

106 Trollope, Anthony. *The West Indies and the Spanish Main*. London, Chapman and Hall, 1860, p.56.

107 Froude, James Anthony. *The English in the West Indies*. London: Longmans, Green and Company, 1888, p.19.

marriage, Mary gave birth to eight children, while Colin ministered to communities at Silver Hill and Clifton, which lie up in the Blue Mountains not far from Raymond Hall. Colin died, aged fifty-one, at the parsonage of his living in Clifton, while Mary lived to be sixty-nine, dying from a broken neck after falling from her horse while riding through Newcastle Cantonment, the hill station built in St Andrew's Parish for British troops stationed in Jamaica.

In 1858 Mary's sister Emily, aged twenty-three, married Major Frederick Cherburgh Bligh, of the Forty-First Regiment of Foot – which had been her father's regiment. Frederick was a member of the wealthy and powerful Bligh family of Brittas Estate in County Meath, Ireland, and it was here that Emily and her husband would live in later life. The couple had four children, one of whom, Ada Theodosia, was born in the Caribbean, on the island of Trinidad. The couple left the Caribbean in later life to live at Brittas, where Emily died at the age of eighty-four. In 1859 Anne's daughter Janetta married Marcus Edmiston Smithett (1831–1885), a commander in the Royal Navy, with whom she returned to England, giving birth to one child, a son, late in 1860.

As both Emily and Janetta married members of the armed forces it is likely that they met their future husbands at one of the balls held regularly in Spanish Town to entertain officers of the navy and the army stationed in Jamaica. These events provided one of the few opportunities for the daughters of the local élite, who often led limited social lives on the rural plantations, to meet a selection of suitable spouses. They were, of course chaperoned, although from a cartoon of a Spanish Town ball held in 1802 it appears that the chaperones – in this case the elderly woman with the annoyed expression in the centre of the group of cavorting girls – found their task a challenge.

The last of Anne's daughters to marry was Isabella, who remained

From: A Grand Jamaica Ball! Or the Creolean Hop... as Exhibeted [sic] in Spanish Town. An 1802 Print from the Library of Congress Collection of British Cartoon Prints.

single until in 1864 – at what would then have been considered the late age of thirty-six – she married the Honourable Oscar Adolphe Yeats Marescaux, President of the Jamaica Chamber of Commerce, Manager of the Colonial Bank in Kingston, and owner of Cherry Hill estate in St Andrew's Parish. Like Trollope and Froude, he held negative views about the recently enslaved, and is quoted as saying: 'Without being forced, the Negro will not work, it is a delusion to think it, it is useless to appeal to his sense of comfort'.[108] Isabella became mistress of Cherry Hill Great House, and there gave birth to a son the year after her marriage. She remained in Jamaica until her death, at the age of seventy-seven, in 1905.

---

108 Bryan, Patrick E. *The Jamaican People, 1880–1902: Race, Class, and Social Control*. London: Macmillan Caribbean, 1991, p.49.

Both of Anne's sons had died at an early age: Francis in 1857, aged nineteen, and Edward in 1862, aged thirty-six, leaving no male heirs to inherit Maryland on the death of Anne's husband in 1866. Anne thus became responsible for running the estate. To succeed in her new role, she would have to make business decisions to ensure the continued profitability of Maryland, a challenge which, as the daughter of Ralph Allen Daniell and granddaughter of Thomas Daniell – both successful businessmen – she may well have relished.

It was, however, a difficult time to manage a coffee plantation. Jamaica's agricultural economy – damaged by low crop prices, droughts, and disease – was declining, while unemployment and the cost of living rose. Voting rights became an increasingly contentious issue as the former enslaved – in theory given the right to vote after full emancipation – realised that in practice the stringent property rules for voters restricted most of them from voting. Social unrest spread throughout the island, and violence began to flare up, culminating, just before Hinton East's death, in the October 1865 Morant Bay Rebellion. Led by Paul Bogle – a native-born Baptist deacon, like Sam Sharpe – the protesting workers marched on the Morant Bay courthouse, where there was a violent confrontation with government forces which left twenty-five people dead and thirty-one injured.

The response from the island's governor, Edward John Eyre, was swift and brutal: the participants were rounded up and 439 were either hanged – including Bogle – or shot by firing squad. Eyre was dismissed from his post, but most wealthy estate owners and their families supported his actions, including Anne Daniell, who – signing herself *Anne East, widow of the late Hon. Hinton East, Member of the Legislative Council*[109] – added her name to a letter of support sent to

---

109 *Jamaica: Addresses to His Excellency Edward John Eyre, Esquire, 1865, 1866.* [Kingston]: M de Cordova and Company, 1866, p.137. Accessed 2 August 2022,

Eyre by 'The Ladies of Jamaica'. Over 3,000 ladies signed the letter. Determined to make their own voices heard rather than rely on the male members of their families to state their views for them, they wrote that:

> *in sincerest regard for your Excellency, we all, Wives, Mothers, Daughters, Widows,[110] offer humble supplication to that Great and Merciful Protector, who, through you, protected us, for every blessing for you, your wife, your children. May He protect and abundantly prosper your future career.[111]*

After the Morant Bay Rebellion Anne Daniell remained in Jamaica, continuing to manage Maryland and to live at Raymond Hall where she died, aged eighty, in 1881.

While Anne chose to stay in Jamaica, many colonists, convinced that there would be further unrest, decided to leave. Among them was a group of Ladies of Quality from Jamaica's plantocracy – widows and an unmarried daughter of independent means – who returned to the Mother Country and settled in and around Penzance. Related by marriage, they were members of the Bryan, Rodon, and Fearon families who owned sugar plantations in the Parish of Clarendon. Only one of the group, Mary Elizabeth Pennant Bryan (1814–1890), had any previous connection with Cornwall. Born in Jamaica, in 1835 she married John Michell – sometimes spelt

---

https://archive.org/stream/jamaicaaddresse00eyregoog/jamaicaaddresse00eyregoog_djvu.txt

110 This part of the quotation – 'Wives, Mothers, Daughters, Widows' – is the source of this book's title.

111 *Jamaica: Addresses to His Excellency Edward John Eyre, Esquire, 1865, 1866.* [Kingston]: M de Cordova and Company, 1866, p.148. Accessed 2 August 2022, https://archive.org/stream/jamaicaaddresse00eyregoog/jamaicaaddresse00eyregoog_djvu.txt

Mitchell or Michelle – who came from Truro. After their marriage Mary and John moved to Ilfracombe, Devon, and here their children were born, but the family later returned to Cornwall, to live in the village of Madron, near Penzance, and here John died, aged forty-six. Mary's mother, Jamaica-born Elizabeth Rodon (1792–1859), joined Mary in Madron after the death of her husband, the Honourable William Pennant Bryan. Mary Burbury McKenzie (1786–1879) was born in the Parish of Vere, Jamaica, married the Reverend George Crawford Ricketts Fearon, the Rector of Vere, and after his death went to live in Penzance with her unmarried daughter, Eliza Oakes Fearon. Following the death of her mother, Eliza's aunt, Mary Rodon – Elizabeth Rodon's sister – came to keep her company in Penzance. When Eliza died, aged eighty-five, she left the considerable sum of £2,992 10s 11d, partly inherited from the compensation her parents had received after the enslaved workers they had owned had been emancipated.[112]

As widows or single women, this group of Penzance Ladies of Quality now had – like Anne Daniell, the Trelawny sisters, Catherine Long, and Margery Price – a level of control over their lives which, as married women subject to the rules of coverture, they had not enjoyed. Although planters and their families returning from the Caribbean colonies frequently settled in London and the home counties, these women chose to live in the far south-west of the country, where the cost of living was lower and their annuities would stretch further to meet their needs. Having spent many years living in the tropical heat of Jamaica, they would have suffered from the cold weather on their return to England and no doubt appreciated the relatively milder climate Cornwall offered. They were also probably acquainted with

---

[112] Information for this paragraph taken from *Legacies of British Slave Ownership*. Accessed throughout 2021 and 2022, https://www.ucl.ac.uk/lbs/

the wealthy Price family of Trengwainton, near Madron, who owned Worthy Park Estate in St Catherine, the neighbouring Parish to Clarendon, where they had once lived, and with whom they could reminisce about their life in Jamaica.

3

The Middling Sort

White women of the Middling Sort belonged to a loosely defined group within the social hierarchy of Britain's colonial enterprise. The most élite members included females who owned, or were members of families who owned, small agricultural enterprises such as coffee estates or livestock farms, and those who belonged to the families of managers of large sugar estates, who came from merchant families, or who were part of the families of professional men such as doctors or lawyers. Women who came lower down in the hierarchy of the group included those from missionary or teaching families, or from the families of the captains of the trading vessels which regularly sailed the seas between the Mother Country and the Caribbean.

One woman born into a Middling Sort of family was Elizabeth Wingfield (1771–1828). Her father, George Wingfield, was a lawyer – a middle-class profession – and her mother, Mary Barkas, was the daughter of one George Sparrow Esquire. But the family moved up the social scale when George's sister Elizabeth married Sir John St Aubyn, 4th Baronet of Clowance, who owned both Clowance Manor in Crowan, a village near Helston, and St Michael's Mount, a small island off the coast of the town of Marazion. Elizabeth's aunt, now Lady Elizabeth St Aubyn, took a great interest in her niece's upbringing; the young Elizabeth frequently spent time in Cornwall with Lady Elizabeth, and over the years came to consider herself a 'Lady of Quality'. In 1797, she married local Cornishman John James (1772–1826) who came from a well-established, although Middling Sort of family. His father was captain of the *Marazion* – a 200-ton merchant ship and privateer,[113] and a liquor merchant who, in his later years, became a farmer, and managed 'a considerable farm'.[114]

Elizabeth Wingfield was a woman of some financial means, and before her marriage to John James she had invested capital in some projects which provided her with dividends. Aware of the precarious financial position of a married woman living under the common law principle of coverture, and determined to keep her financial independence, she had an agreement drawn up between herself and her husband-to-be – a 'retain indenture' – whereby after marriage she kept the capital she had invested, and continued to benefit from the dividends from her investments.[115]

Soon after her marriage Elizabeth gave birth to a daughter, Elizabeth Prideaux, who was born in 1798. A son, John Wingfield, was born in 1800, and a second daughter, Mary, followed in 1801. The family lived comfortably in a large house in Marazion, and Elizabeth and her husband seemed destined to live out their lives as respected members of the local community, enjoying the lively society of the nearby town of Penzance until in 1803 Elizabeth's husband was offered the post of manager of an agricultural estate

---

113 The National Archives of the UK. Public Record Office. *High Court of Admiralty: Prize Court: Registers of Declarations for Letters of Marque.* HCA26/6/123.

114 'Suddenly at St Michael's Mount, near Marazion, Captain John James, aged about 80.' *The Monthly Register and Encyclopedian Magazine*, pp.47–48. Accessed 7 March 2022, https://babel.hathitrust.org/cgi/pt?id=uiug.30112098086371&view=1up&seq=60&skin=2021&q1=Captain%20John%20James

115 From correspondence with Maxine Symons and Kyle Scott, February 2022.

on the island of Barbuda by the estate's owner, Sir Christopher Bethel Codrington.

The Codrington family had first come to the Caribbean in 1649, and over the years had become wealthy and influential estate owners on the islands of Barbados, Antigua, Barbuda, and Tobago. Later generations of the family, including Sir Christopher, who lived at Dodington Park, the family estate in Gloucestershire, preferred the life of an absentee planter, and employed managers to run their Caribbean estates.

After mulling over Sir Christopher's offer of an annual salary of £200 plus a 5 per cent commission on profit from the sale of Barbuda's products, John decided in 1804 to accept the post of manager of the Barbuda estate and, leaving his family behind in Marazion, he sailed for Antigua and on to Barbuda, where he set about developing the estate in a businesslike manner. Unlike the Codrington sugar estates on Barbados, Antigua, and Tobago, the Barbuda property had initially been developed as a stock-rearing facility to supply the Codrington estates on Antigua with meat and draught animals, but production later diversified to include hides, sheep wool, corn, wood, charcoal, lime – used in the production of sugar – fish, and the meat and shells of turtles.[116] As production increased the estate began to supply a wider market, including the Royal Navy's base at English Harbour on the south coast of Antigua, and neighbouring islands, while wool, cotton, and turtle shells were occasionally sent as far as England.[117] An additional and significant source of the estate's income was the salvaging of the vessels that frequently ran aground on the reefs that

---

116 Tweedy, Margaret T. 'A History of Barbuda Under the Codringtons 1738–1833.' PhD diss., University of Birmingham, 1981, p.i. Accessed 11 February 2022, https://etheses.bham.ac.uk/id/eprint/5356/.

117 Watters, David R. 'Observations on the Historic Sites and Archaeology of Barbuda.' *Journal of Archaeology and Anthropology*, pp.125–156 (Vol.3, No.2, 1980).

surround the low-lying island, and as a Cornish man from the often-treacherous coast of Cornwall, whose rocky coastline and strong onshore winds cause many vessels to founder, John James would have possessed the skills needed to successfully salvage shipwrecks.

Sir Christopher was initially pleased with the efforts of his new employee to improve his property, and a year later gave him additional financial responsibilities and power of attorney to act for the Barbuda estate.[118] But by 1809 Sir Christopher's enthusiasm for John's efforts had faded, and he complained that his Barbuda investments were not bringing an adequate return. Many absentee planters tended to blame the local manager for any shortfall in profit, and Sir Christopher was no exception, failing to consider the ongoing challenges of Barbuda's poor soil and the frequent shortage of water, and the difficulty of maintaining regular communication between Barbuda and the Codrington country estate in Gloucestershire.

In 1815 John travelled to England on plantation business and to visit his family. Elizabeth had been left to manage the family's affairs in Cornwall during the eleven years her husband had been employed on Barbuda, but she now apparently wanted to join her husband; on John's return to the island he asked Sir Christopher's permission to bring his wife and two daughters out to Barbuda.[119] Sir Christopher agreed to the arrangement, and the three women sailed for Barbuda. It is uncertain exactly when they left Marazion, but it must have been after Elizabeth had advertised their house as a rental property in the *Royal Cornwall Gazette* for Saturday 17 May 1817:

---

118 *The Letters of John James Esq.: A Collection of Letters Written by the Estate Manager of Barbuda and Clare Hall, Antigua 1804–1826*. Accessed 7 March 2022, http://johnjamesesq.blogspot.com/2013/10/02-august-1805.html

119 Tweedy, Margaret T. 'A History of Barbuda Under the Codringtons 1738–1833.' PhD diss., University of Birmingham, 1981, p.58. Accessed 11 February 2022, https://etheses.bham.ac.uk/id/eprint/5356/

To be LET, WITH IMMEDIATE Possession, A READY-FURNISHED HOUSE, Delightfully situated in the Centre of MARAZION. The house consists of Two Parlours, a Drawing-Room, Six Bed-Rooms, a Kitchen, Wash Kitchen, Dairy, Coach-House, Stables, and a good Pump, etc. etc. with walled Garden. Apply to Mrs. James at Marazion. Dated 13 May, 1817.[120]

Elizabeth's son, John Wingfield, did not accompany them. He was a student at Blundell's School in Tiverton, Devon, from 1814 to 1815,[121] and as he was the only male heir his father no doubt thought it important that he continue his schooling in England rather than accompany his mother and sisters to Barbuda. He is, however, thought to have gone out to spend time with his family in 1823, when he was about twenty-three years old.[122]

The usual residence for Barbuda's estate manager was Codrington Castle, built in 1680 to defend the island against attacks from opposing European colonists and marauding pirates. By the time John James arrived the village of Codrington had grown up around the castle, which was then mainly used for storing the estate's supplies and salvage items. The castle's living quarters, situated in the lower part of the building, were said to be damp, and by 1813 the castle was described as run down and 'dilapidated'.[123]

---

120 'To be Let…' *Royal Cornwall Gazette*, p.1. (Saturday 7 May 1817)
121 *The Register of Blundell's School Part 1: The Register 1770–1882*. Exeter: J.G. Commin, 1904, p.87. Accessed 7 March 2022, https://forgottenbooks.com/it/download/TheRegisterofBlundellsSchool_10913062.pdf
122 Estate records list John Wingfield as an employee on the property for at least three months in 1823. From correspondence with Maxine Symon and Kyle Scott, February 2022.
123 Tweedy, Margaret T. 'A History of Barbuda Under the Codringtons 1738–1833.' PhD diss., University of Birmingham, 1981, p.170. Accessed 11 February 2022,

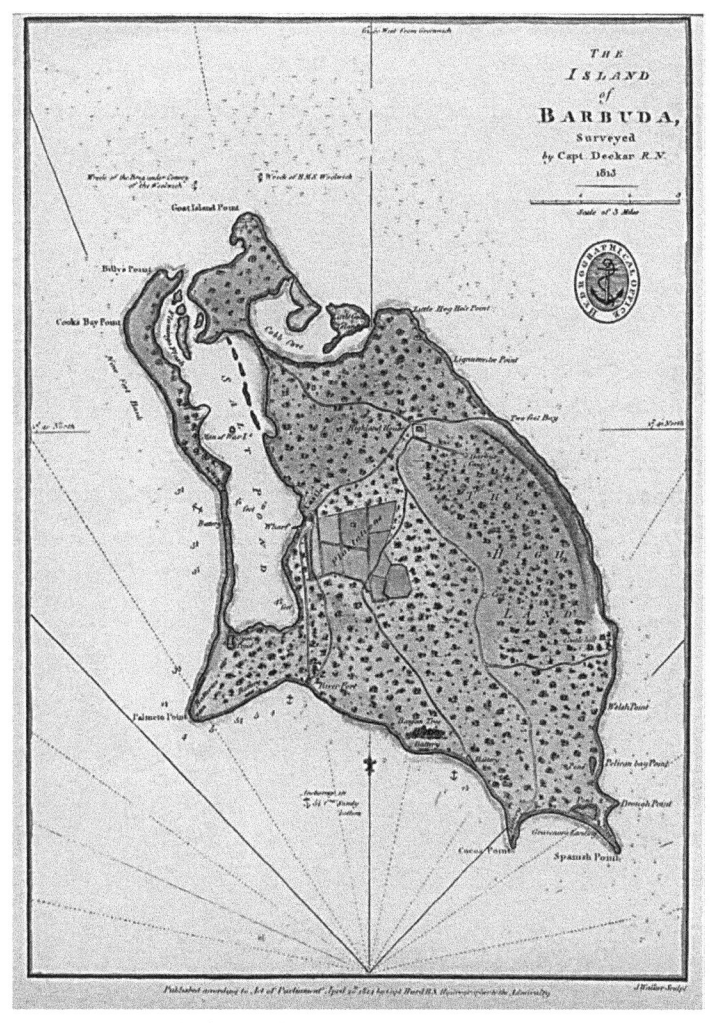

A Map of the Island of Barbuda, by Captain Decker, Royal Navy, 1813.

By the time Elizabeth and her two daughters arrived on Barbuda in 1817, John had wisely moved from the castle to a 'large barn-like

---

https://etheses.bham.ac.uk/id/eprint/5356/.

looking house'[124] which had been built nearby and provided more comfortable accommodation. What Elizabeth and her daughters thought of the house is not recorded, but it surely did not compare favourably to the house they left behind in Marazion. What they thought of life on Barbuda is also unknown, but Codrington village was – and indeed still is – the only centre of population on the island. It was the estate's administrative centre, where the enslaved workers and overseers were housed, and was also the location of facilities such as the tannery, where hides from the island's livestock were processed and where the stench produced by the tanning process would have been inescapable.[125] Unless the family travelled to Antigua there was no opportunity for socialising with managers and families of neighbouring estates, so John's family most likely found Barbuda a lonely place to live, and missed the social life they had enjoyed in Marazion and Penzance.

There is only one known pictorial representation of Codrington from the time of the James family's residence on Barbuda: a watercolour entitled *A View of the Island of Barbuda in the West Indies*. Completed in 1818, it includes one wall of the castle to the left of the painting and, in the centre, what is probably the 'barn-like house'[126] where the James family were living. The name of the painter is written on the back as 'N. James' but could this be 'M. James' – for Mary James?[127] Mary was living on Barbuda when the painting was made, and there is no evidence that any member of the James family

---

124 Ibid., p.170.
125 Watters, David R. 'Observations on the Historic Sites and Archaeology of Barbuda.' *Journal of Archaeology and Anthropology*, pp.125–156 (Vol.3, No.2, 1980), p.232.
126 This house, now known as Government House or the Warden's House, was built in about 1694. When the Codrington family left Barbuda in 1870, it became the residence of the warden – the representative of the British government on Barbuda.
127 Information supplied by Elizabeth Shannon, Hamilton College, in email message of 21 February 2022.

A View of the Island of Barbuda in the West Indies, by N. James, 1818. Courtesy of the Ruth and Elmer Wellin Museum of Art, Hamilton College, Clinton, New York, USA.

with a first name beginning with an N ever resided on Barbuda.[128] Was Mary, then aged seventeen, a budding artist? Did she begin to draw and paint to pass the time while she was living in the village of Codrington? If it is her painting, it is the only known artwork she produced.

In 1822 John, in addition to his responsibilities on Barbuda, was made manager of Clare Hall sugar estate on Antigua, a property recently bought by Sir Christopher. The Clare Hall Great House was an elegant building surrounded by mature trees which self-described Lady of Quality Mrs Carmichael had visited some

---

128 Confirmed in email message from Kyle Scott dated 15 March 2022, based on his research for *The Letters of John James Esq.: A Collection of Letters Written by the Estate Manager of Barbuda and Clare Hall, Antigua 1804–1826* – http://johnjamesesq.blogspot.com/p/blog-page_2030.html and his search of the 1817 Slave Register for Barbuda, which provides names of the Codrington slaves on Barbuda and did not show any slave with the James surname.

years earlier and found to be: 'superb [and the grounds] laid out with groves and delightful walks of tamarind trees, which give the finest shade you can imagine.'[129] Given the living conditions on Barbuda, Elizabeth and her daughters unsurprisingly now made their principal home at Clare Hall, a residence which would have been more to their liking than the barn-like house in Codrington. As opportunities for socialising improved, Elizabeth – perhaps remembering the life she had lived as a young girl at Clowance Manor and St Michael's Mount – began to renovate the house and entertain on a grand scale.

The attorney for the Codrington estates on Antigua, a Mr Osborn, wrote to Sir Christopher about Elizabeth's extravagant behaviour: 'Mrs James has eighteen people waiting on her besides one of the head carpenters constantly at the house and a stout woman every day out of the field to wash the house.'[130] Osborn also noted that Mrs James kept between five and seven horses, which had to be cared for and which were fed four quarts of corn each per day, and that she held regular large parties for 'eighty able people.'[131] As Sir Christopher was responsible for paying any debts incurred by the James family, he was understandably displeased with the amount of money they were now spending, and he writes:

> I have to observe that until Mrs James took up her abode in the W. Indies, my property under her husband's management was set to give me a handsome annual income. From that period it would

---

[129] Carmichael, A.C. *Domestic Manners and Social Condition of the White, Coloured and Negro Population of the West Indies*. 2 vols. London: Whittaker Treacher and Co., 1833, p.83.

[130] *Letters from Christopher Bethel Codrington to John James [and family]*. Gloucestershire Records Office, D1610 C24. Accessed 29 August 2022, https://digital.lib.sfu.ca/cwc-97/letters-christopher-bethell-codrington-john-james?search=John%2520James

[131] Ibid.

have been better for me to have had no such property. I have at this moment in my hands debts contracted by him or her amounting to 4000 and upward for the payment of which I have accepted bills.[132]

Now usually to be found with his family at Clare Hall, John James, who had been in poor health for some time, was unable to manage the Codrington affairs as he once had. During 1826 his health continued to decline, and at the end of July of that year he died at Clare Hall, leaving his business affairs unsettled. He is buried in the churchyard of St John the Divine Cathedral in St John's, Antigua.

Elizabeth and her daughters returned to England after John's death, and on arriving in London Elizabeth began to correspond with Sir Christopher concerning the settlement of outstanding payments relating to her husband's employment. She is not intimidated by Sir Christopher, and her letter is businesslike in tone:

> I have the honour of enclosing a memorandum of Mr James last year superintendence [sic] of Barbuda. I have left *that* island totally unencumbered of debt up to my melancholy loss, and flatter myself you will find it correct. I beg leave to inform you that Mr James has… never received his commissions on wool, cotton and turtle shell that has been sent to England for sale from time to time.[133]

Leaving London, Elizabeth returned to Cornwall, but she became unwell in the early months of 1828, and in late May, before she was able to bring her correspondence with Sir Christopher to a satisfactory conclusion, she died at the house in Marazion. Her

---

132 Ibid.
133 Ibid.

body was placed in the Wingfield family mausoleum in Crowan churchyard, a high-status interment which would surely have pleased her.[134] [135] She must have been aware that her health was deteriorating because – preparing for the future as she had done when she had drawn up the pre-nuptial agreement with her husband – she wrote her will two months before her death. In it she gives clear instructions that the sum of her capital investments, totalling the considerable sum of £7,700, is to be divided equally between her two daughters, who would be able to live comfortably on the dividends. Elizabeth also left her daughters her freehold lands and everything on them, and her furniture and other household possessions. Thanks to her successful circumvention of the constraints of coverture Elizabeth had succeeded in keeping control of her financial capital and in passing it on to her daughters. She would have been expected to leave the bulk of her wealth to the only male heir, her son John Wingfield – but he only received a bequest of £300. Did mother and son fall out? It cannot be that he married into a wealthy family so had no need of a larger inheritance, as he is recorded as having worked as a customs officer in London after his marriage.[136]

After Elizabeth's death the correspondence concerning the financial disagreement between Sir Christopher and the James family was taken up by Elizabeth's daughter Mary. In November 1828 she writes to Sir Christopher that, the family 'being now anxious to settle and furnish a house which from want of spare cash we have not been

---

134 Symons, Maxine. 'Bring up the Bodies: Digging up the Truth in the Lost Mausoleum at Crowan.' *Journal of the Royal Institution of Cornwall*, pp.10–33 (2021).

135 The Wingfield mausoleum at Crowan was subsequently demolished, and the current burial site of the bodies it contained, including that of Elizabeth Wingfield, is unmarked.

136 Information for this paragraph is based on email correspondence with Kyle Scott and Maxine Symons, February and October 2022.

able to accomplish,'[137] she wishes the outstanding payments to be made by Sir Christopher to the family. Presumably she and her sister had not received the first payment of the dividends on her mother's investments when she wrote this letter, and they were therefore short of ready cash. When Mary hears of Mr Osborn's report to Sir Christopher concerning her parents' extravagant lifestyle, she angrily refutes the accusation, writing to Sir Christopher:

> *We regret exceedingly the misrepresentations that have been made to you respecting both our departed parents, having always understood that our dear father came into the management of Clare Hall when much encumbered with debts (some thousands) [and] that at the time of his desease [sic] there remained but a small portion of this to pay (only a few hundred). It is indeed very unfair… to make any remarks on Mrs. James parties as they were very scarce – one quadrille party a year only and half a dozen dinner parties during the same space of time.*[138]

The correspondence now peters out. As the sisters came into their inheritance and began to receive their dividends they found themselves financially well off, and perhaps the matter of chasing after monies they believed were owing to their parents became less urgent. The elder sister, Elizabeth Prideaux, married George Mortimer, a retired Royal Navy lieutenant, and settled in Devon, where she gave birth to a son, William Bassett Mortimer. Mary seems not to have married and to have remained in Cornwall until her death.[139]

---

137 *Letters from Christopher Bethel Codrington to John James [and family].* Gloucestershire Records Office, D1610 C24. Accessed 29 August 2022, https://digital.lib.sfu.ca/cwc-97/letters-christopher-bethell-codrington-john-james?search=John%2520James
138 Ibid.
139 Information for this paragraph taken from correspondence with Kyle Scott and

A near-contemporary of Elizabeth Wingfield was Eliza Jaco (1766–1840) who came from a Middling Sort of family much lower down the social scale than the Wingfields; Eliza's father, Peter Jaco, who worked for the family pilchard fishery business in Newlyn,[140] was one of John Wesley's early followers and became an itinerant Methodist lay preacher. From about 1755 until his death in London in 1781 he travelled widely to various Methodist circuits in England, so it is uncertain exactly where Eliza was born, but after her father's death she probably lived with her widowed mother in London. Here she met John Fenwick, whose father was, like her own father, an itinerant Methodist lay preacher.[141] John was a political radical and writer and occasional translator and journalist with a reputation for being a heavy drinker and a spendthrift. He was a friend of William Godwin, the journalist and political philosopher, whose wife, the writer and advocate of women's rights, Mary Wollstonecraft, became a close friend of Eliza. A teacher in her early adult life, Wollstonecraft was the author of *A Vindication of the Rights of Woman*,[142] which argued that an educational system that allowed girls the same advantages as boys would produce women who would be capable both of being wives and mothers and of earning a living by working.

Through Godwin and Wollstonecraft, Eliza met other members of the group, including Charles and Mary Lamb, Thomas Holcroft, Crabb Robinson, and Mary Hays, who all

---

Maxine Symons, February and October 2022.
140 MacKenzie, Charlotte. *Cornish Connections with 1790s Radical and Literary Circles: Part 1*, p.9. Accessed 24 September 2021, http://cornishstory.com/2019/04/07/cornish-connections-with-1790s-radical-and-literary-circles/
141 Ibid., pp.1–3.
142 Wollstonecraft, Mary. *A Vindication of the Rights of Woman*. Accessed 2 September 2022, https://www.gutenberg.org/ebooks/3420

believed in the ideals of liberty and equality, and supported the abolition of slavery. Eliza became especially close to Mary Hays, and corresponded with her throughout her adult life. Hays argued strongly for recognition of the rational qualities of women, the necessity of a better system of education for girls, and the importance of giving women without fortunes a career so they would not have to turn to prostitution. Here was an educated woman who managed to make at least some financial profit from her writing, and Eliza, who had perhaps already realised she could not rely on John Fenwick to provide for the family – which now included the couple's daughter, Eliza Ann, born in 1789 – turned her hand to writing to supplement the family income. In common with Wollstonecraft's *Maria: or, the Wrongs of Woman*[143] and Hays' *The Victim of Prejudice*,[144] Fenwick's 1795 novel, *Secresy or the Ruin on the Rock*,[145] illustrates the various forms of oppression experienced by women in patriarchal society.

Following the birth of her son Orlando in 1798, Eliza's relationship with John Fenwick may have briefly become more stable, but over the next few years John continued to fall deeper into debt, borrowing money he could not repay when his attempts at business ventures failed. In 1802 Eliza decided to leave him and move to Cornwall. Several factors influenced her decision: members of her father's family who might offer her their support lived in the Mount's Bay area; a brother-in-law, Thomas Fenwick, owned a draper's shop in Penzance, where she might find employment; and the poor health of her daughter, Eliza Ann, who she was advised would benefit from the mild climate of Penzance.

---

143 Wollstonecraft, Mary. *Maria: Or, the Wrongs of Woman.* New York: Norton, 1975.
144 Hays, Mary. *The Victim of Prejudice.* 2nd ed. Peterborough: Broadview Press, 1998.
145 Fenwick, Eliza. *Secresy or the Ruin on the Rock.* Peterborough: Broadview Press, 1994.

The move was initially successful: Eliza enjoyed roaming the Cornish countryside, her daughter's health improved sufficiently for her to attend school in Falmouth, and Thomas Fenwick was happy to give his sister-in-law a job in his shop. Unfortunately, however, by the middle of 1803 the shop was losing money and Thomas was declared bankrupt so, unable to make a living in Penzance, Eliza returned to London, where she now began to write children's books.

Over the next few years she published ten titles,[146] including *Visits to the Juvenile Library; or, Knowledge Proved to be the Source of Happiness*, in which she writes about the education of Nora, an enslaved woman. The book tells the story of five orphaned children who, accompanied by Nora, are sent to England from their home in the Caribbean to live with their guardian, a Mrs Clifford. The children are unhappy and badly behaved, but when they learn to read they become model children. Nora notices the positive effect that learning to read has had on their behaviour and begins to teach herself to read. When two of the children surprise her as she is at work on her spelling, she tells them:

> *Well me tell all–you, Massa Henry, was cross boy, sometimes cruel boy to poor Nora – you, Massa Arthur, use to call Nora here, send Nora there; never satisfied if Nora sat down a moment, and you sit still and scold all day. Since you come to England, you get books, you read books, you talk together, play together, read again, play again, be happy, be merry, fetch your own play-things, put them away, no call poor old Nora down stairs, up stairs, now pick up a*

---

146 MacKenzie, Charlotte. *Cornish Connections with 1790s Radical and Literary Circles: Part 1*, p.10. Accessed 24 September 2021, http://cornishstory.com/2019/04/07/cornish-connections-with-1790s-radical-and-literary-circles/

Nora Endeavouring to Read. From: Fenwick, Eliza. *A Visit to the Juvenile Library*. London: Tabard, 1805. Courtesy of the New York Public Library Digital Collections.

ball, now to tie your shoes, no scold and quarrel with Nora when you go to bed; all kind and good to Nora now. Nora think you have learn it all out of books, so Nora learn books too.[147]

A Visit to the Juvenile Library shows that Eliza was aware both of the importance of education for girls and women, including the enslaved, and that she knew, to some extent at least, of the treatment enslaved people received in the colonial society, of which she disapproved. While Eliza continued to write, she recognised that writing alone did not bring her enough income to support her two

---

147 Immel, Andrea. *An Enslaved Woman Learns to Read in Eliza Fenwick's A Visit to the Juvenile Library (1805)*. Accessed 12 September 2022, https://blogs.princeton.edu/cotsen/tag/enslaved-people/.

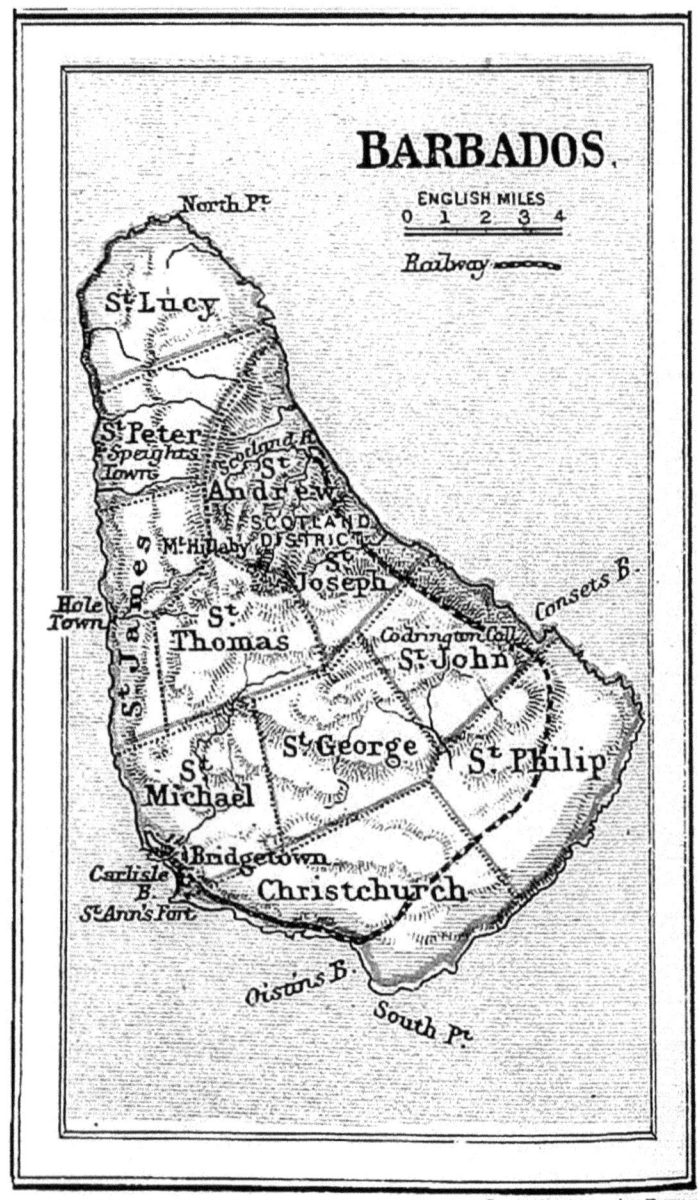

A Map of the Island of Barbados. From: Lucas, C.P. Historical Geography of the British Colonies. Vol 2. Oxford: Clarendon Press, 1888, p.158.

children and herself, and in 1812 she accepted the post of governess to a family who lived near Cork in Ireland.

Meanwhile Eliza's daughter, after considering a teaching career, had established herself as an actor on the London stage. Her career was progressing well, but in 1811 she failed to secure any suitable acting parts for the upcoming London season. Now out of work and with no regular income, she was ready to consider an invitation from a Barbados entrepreneur – one Mr Dyke – to join the company of actors who would open his new theatre in Bridgetown, Barbados. After considerable discussion with her mother, Eliza Ann decided to accept Mr Dyke's proposal. The plan, they agreed, was for her to travel to Barbados, where her contract fee would enable her to earn enough money to pay for her mother and brother to join her. Then, once established in Barbados, Eliza, encouraged by her friend Mary Hays to provide an educational opportunity for the girls on the island, would open a school for girls.

Soon after arriving in Barbados, Eliza Ann met William Rutherford, a fellow actor. The couple married the following year, and in 1813 Eliza Ann gave birth to their first child, William Patrick. By 1814 there were sufficient funds available to pay for Eliza and Orlando's passage to Barbados, a destination which on arrival Eliza found to be a 'Land of Promise'.[148] Excited about her future, she wrote enthusiastically to Mary Hays: 'Our prospects, I am assured, are excellent, and… Eliza [Ann] and Mr. Rutherford are no less sanguine on the subject.'[149]

Full of optimism, Eliza soon established a small school for girls in Barbados. To support her family, she needed pupils whose families

---

148 Fenwick, Eliza. *The Fate of the Fenwicks: Letters to Mary Hays (1798–1828)*. London: Methuen, 1927, p.163.
149 Ibid., p.165.

could pay her a substantial fee to educate their daughters – the wealthy local plantocracy – and, with the teaching assistance of her daughter and son-in-law she was able to offer a wide selection of subjects which proved popular with the clientèle she wished to attract. Within six months of opening the school had thirty pupils, and parents were requesting that she take in boarders. Her prices were higher than the other schools on the island which, she wrote Hays, encouraged those from 'the higher and wealthy classes'[150] to send their daughters to the school, often as an alternative to sending them to England.

In order to earn a living Eliza now seems to have put any radical thoughts she may have had on universal education out of her mind. She is focused on educating the daughters of wealthy colonists, although she still expresses her anti-slavery views quite strongly when in March 1815 she writes to Mary Hays that slavery:

> *is a horrid and disgraceful system. The female slaves are really encouraged to prostitution because their children are the property of the owner of the mothers… What is still more horrible, the Gentlemen are greatly addicted to their women slaves, and give the fruit of their licentiousness to their white children as slaves… It gives me disgusted antipathy and I am ready to hail the Slave and reject the Master.*[151]

But her words are not supported by her actions. As she writes about her abhorrence of slavery, she is hiring enslaved women to run her household. Did she believe what she wrote to Hays, or did she write what she thought Hays would want to hear? Eliza justified her use of enslaved women by stating that they were an

---

150 Ibid., p.167.
151 Ibid., p.169.

inferior race, and wrote to Hays – who must have been surprised to receive this new correspondence so at odds with her friend's professed horror of slavery – that they were inferior to 'even the worst of English servants... a sluggish, inert, self-willed race of people.'[152] Supposedly ready to 'hail the slave', Eliza totally fails to understand the impact the slavery system has on the behaviour of the enslaved and how their only means of resistance – other than running away – was limited to performing their tasks in a 'sluggish' and 'inert' manner. In common with the plantocracy who supplied her school with paying pupils, and to whose views on slavery she no doubt listened, she instead ascribes this behaviour to negative racial characteristics.

Tension between the enslaved and their owners was endemic to the system of slavery, but Eliza's arrival on Barbados coincided with an increase in that tension that was the result of two events: the success of the rebellion in French-owned Saint-Domingue which, having begun in 1791, had culminated in the colony's independence as Haiti in 1804, and the growing strength of the anti-slavery movement, which led to the abolition of the transatlantic trade in enslaved Africans in 1807. Both events brought the possibility of emancipation closer and encouraged the enslaved to increase their efforts to secure their freedom. In Barbados the growing discontent erupted in April 1816, when the enslaved put into action a well-organised plan to destroy plantations and attack the local militia. Known as the Easter Rebellion or Bussa's Rebellion – after an African-born man, Bussa, one of the leaders of the rebellion – it was swiftly put down with great ferocity but nevertheless left the colonists in fear of subsequent uprisings.

Eliza reported that the rebellion terrified her, made her seriously ill and caused her business to lose income, as many members of

---

152 Ibid., p.163.

the plantocracy, having had their sugar crop and much of their infrastructure destroyed, either left the island with their families or could no longer afford to send their daughters to her school.[153] Worse was to come. In October 1816 a hurricane passed over the island and damaged much of Bridgetown and the surrounding areas; and a month later Eliza's son Orlando died from yellow fever. Meanwhile, Eliza's daughter Eliza Ann was in poor health and in 1818, having given birth to four children in six years, was deserted by her husband, William Rutherford, who – much like Eliza's husband – was a heavy drinker and ran up substantial debts he was unable to repay.[154]

Eliza remained optimistic that her school would continue to bring in a profit, but the cost of hiring enslaved males and females continued to be of financial concern to her, and she now turned to ownership as a more economical way of running her business.

She writes to Mary Hays:

Upwards of a year since, I hired a very excellent Cook of a Widow Lady, and soon after I had him, she pressed me to purchase him. As he suited us particularly well and had fewer faults and evil propensities than most of the black servants, …I took him, at £140… It will no doubt be repugnant to your feelings to hear me talk of **buying** *Men. It was for a long time revolting to mine, but the heavy Sums we have paid for wages of hired servants, who were generally the most worthless of their kind, rendered it necessary. Out of the 8 in our household, 5 are now our property, 2 men, 2 boys and one woman.*[155]

---

153 Rosenthal, Jamie. 'From Radical Feminist to Caribbean Slave Owner: Eliza Fenwick's Barbados Letters.' *Eighteenth-Century Studies*, p.62 (Vol.52, No. 1, 2018).

154 Ibid., p.57.

155 Fenwick, Eliza. *The Fate of the Fenwicks: Letters to Mary Hays (1798–1828)*. London: Methuen, 1927, p.207.

Eliza's ownership of a small number of enslaved people was not unusual. As the owner of a school in Bridgetown, she was representative of the small-business culture of towns across the Caribbean, where middle-class white and freed women often owned small properties and enterprises, and either hired or owned a few enslaved people.[156]

We do not know how Eliza treated her enslaved workers, although middle-class women could, like mistresses of the plantation Great Houses, treat them harshly, showing little sign of the supposed gentle and restrained behaviour expected of the 'fairer sex'. Mary Prince, an enslaved women born on Bermuda, was one of the few to tell of her abusive experience after she had been sold to new owners in Spanish Point, Bermuda. Her new mistress, she writes:

> *taught me to do all sorts of household work; to wash and bake, pick cotton and wool, and wash floors and cook. And she taught me (how can I ever forget it!) more things than these; she caused me to know the exact difference between the smart of the rope, the cart-whip, and the cow skin*[157] *when applied to my naked body by her own cruel hand. And there was scarcely any punishment more dreadful than the blows I received on my face and head from her hard heavy fist. She was a fearful woman, and a savage mistress to her slaves.*[158]

Although Eliza's school in Barbados continued to be a moderate success, Eliza and her daughter, now with four children to support,

---

156 Beckles, Hilary MacDonald. *Centering Women: Gender Discourses in Caribbean Slave Society*. Kingston: Ian Randle, 1999, p.79.
157 A long flexible whip made of cow skin.
158 Jones, Cecily. *Engendering Whiteness: White Women and Colonialism in Barbados and North Carolina, 1627–1865*. Manchester: Manchester University Press, 2014, p.206.

began to discuss the possibility of leaving Barbados and moving to New Haven, Connecticut, where, they had been told, there were good prospects for setting up a school for girls. Eliza writes to Mary Hays:

> Three years have now elapsed since Mr. Rutherford left the Island, and we are perfect strangers to his fate… I am pleased on this account with our project of removal, because I can look for a lasting settlement for Eliza in America. I should die here with a painful impression of the various disasters that might overwhelm her and her children in sudden ruin, – our storms, – our hurricanes, – but above all the fatal insurrection which we constantly dread, prevent the soothing consciousness of being at home.[159]

In 1821, after ten years in Barbados, Eliza and her daughter sold their property and, with Eliza Anne's four children, moved to New Haven, where once again Eliza enthusiastically embarked on a project to teach the daughters of the wealthy citizens of the town. She writes to Hays:

> There happens to be no female school of the higher order at New-Haven, though several at New York, and it is supposed that ours would be very attractive, as the principal families are now compelled to engage Masters at home.[160]

Strangely – in a woman supposedly devoted to improving female education – she advises Hays that one of the main advantages

---

159 Fenwick, Eliza. *The Fate of the Fenwicks: Letters to Mary Hays (1798–1828)*. London: Methuen, 1927, pp.212–213.
160 Ibid., p.210.

of moving to the mainland is not the opportunity to educate girls but 'the opportunity of giving excellent education to our boys and bringing them up to habits of industry and utility at a very moderate expense.'[161]

Eliza's efforts to support herself and her family continued to meet setbacks, as Eliza Anne, who frequently suffered from ill health, died in New York in 1827, leaving Eliza to bring up her four grandchildren. To make ends meet Eliza continued to teach, even if she now gave little thought to the feminist and radical beliefs she had apparently held as a young woman. She tried many ways to make a living for herself and her family throughout her life, and her great-great niece commented on her inability to focus on one course of action for any length of time:

> *recklessly impulsive... She tries in turn writing, school-keeping, helping in her brother-in-law's shop, ...acting as resident governess... A chance piece of advice, the casual suggestion of an acquaintance, is enough to change the mind of this weather-cock woman.*[162]

Eliza died in 1840, in Providence, Rhode Island, a few years after the passing of Britain's Emancipation Act of 1833. What were her views on emancipation? Rhode Island emancipated the enslaved members of its population in 1844, and Connecticut in 1848, but the United States did not abolish slavery at the Federal level until 1863 – well after her death. Once she had left the Caribbean did this 'weather-cock woman' continue to justify her past ownership of enslaved people, or did she return to her earlier professed hatred of the system?

---

161 Ibid., pp.210–211.
162 Ibid., p.x.

Like Eliza, Jane Wright (1836–1921) came from a Cornish family with roots in the Mount's Bay area. They were from Mousehole,[163] a coastal village near to Penzance that had been an important fishing port since the 13th century. Jane's family, like Eliza's, were of the Middling Sort. They were staunch supporters of Wesleyan Methodism, and when a Methodist chapel was established in Mousehole in 1825, the trustees included Jane's father, her grandfather, and two of her uncles. On her mother's side of the family her great-grandfather was a ship's pilot, one of 'His Majesty's Pilots for the Coasts of Cornwall and the Scilly Isles', and her grandfather was both a respected navigator and a poet.[164] On leaving school, Jane earned a living as a dressmaker, living with her parents in Mousehole, where her social life was largely centred on events organised by the local Methodist Society and where she probably met local seaman Henry Blewett (1836–1891).

Henry's early working days had been spent with the Mousehole fishing fleet but, having decided he wanted to see more of the world, he left Mousehole to join the Merchant Navy as an ordinary seaman. In 1860 he returned to Mousehole to marry Jane and begin the course of study that would lead to his promotion to Master Mariner. He joined Scruttons, a London-based firm of ship owners and insurance brokers that had partnerships with prominent Caribbean sugar producers and merchants, relationships that helped the company prosper as it ensured both a market for Scruttons goods in the Caribbean and a ready cargo of sugar products available for the return voyage.[165]

---

163 Pronounced 'Mousle', to rhyme with 'tousle'.
164 Parsons, Jack, and Nora Parsons. *Cornish Fisherboy to Master Mariner: The Life of Henry Blewett 1836–1891. Part One 1836–1861: Mousehole Boyhood and Early Days at Sea.* Bournemouth: Bournemouth Local Studies Publications, 1993, pp.49–51.
165 Appleby, Sue. *The Cornish in the Caribbean: From the 17th to the 19th Centuries.*

With London his home port, Henry first sailed to British Guiana – now Guyana – and the island of Dominica[166] while Jane – now with two baby daughters, Eliza Jane and Mary Wright – continued to live in Mousehole. But when Henry qualified as a Master Mariner in 1864 and Scruttons offered him a permanent ship's captain position, Jane and the children left Mousehole to set up home in London, where they joined the small community of families of Cornish men working for Scruttons, living in Bromehead Street in Stepney.[167] Here a first son, Henry Michael, was born.

In 1866 Henry was given command of the barque *Roseau*,[168] a ship he would captain for the next fifteen years. St Vincent became his regular port of call, and between 1866 and 1881 he made thirty-five voyages to the island. Meanwhile Jane moved to a larger house in nearby Gardom Street, where a third daughter, Rosea Henrietta – called after her father's ship – and a second son, Charles Alexander, were born. With her husband usually away Jane was responsible, with the help of her younger sister Elizabeth, for managing the Blewett household, which by the early 1870s included two lodgers, who provided an additional source of income.[169]

Kibworth Beauchamp: Matador, 2019, p.152.

166 Pronounced with the stress on the third syllable – DominEEca – as against the Dominican Republic, which shares the island of Hispaniola with Haiti, and whose stress is on the second syllable: DoMINican.

167 Parsons, Jack, and Nora Parsons. Cornish Fisherboy to Master Mariner: *The Life of Henry Blewett 1836–1891. Part Two 1861–1866: Mate and Master Mariner.* Bournemouth: Bournemouth Local Studies Publications, 1993, p.34.

168 The 371-ton barque *Roseau* was built on the island of Jersey in 1857 by the firm of F.C. Clarke. Her original restored figurehead now stands at De Bradley Wharf in Dover, Kent, and a replica is on display in the Museum of the Heritage Trust in St Helier, Jersey.

169 Parsons, Jack, and Nora Parsons. *Cornish Fisherboy to Master Mariner: The Life of Henry Blewett 1836–1891. Part Two 1861–1866: Mate and Master Mariner.* Bournemouth: Bournemouth Local Studies Publications, 1993, p.43.

Map of the Island of St Vincent. From: Lucas, C. P. *Historical Geography of the British Colonies*. Vol 2. Oxford: Clarendon Press, 1888, p.227.

Jane's life took on a new dimension when she and the children began to join Henry on many of his voyages to and from St Vincent. In spite of the old superstition that a woman on board brought bad luck to a ship, by the mid-19th century it was not unusual for a woman to join her husband at sea when he was captain of one of the merchant ships sailing the world's trade routes.[170] These women, who sailed on voyages that were often long and difficult and sometimes dangerous, called themselves 'sister sailors', and a ship with the captain's wife or daughter aboard was known as a 'Hen Frigate' – even if the ship was not actually a frigate.[171] It was a term coined by crews to describe any vessel in which it was thought that the wife or daughter interfered with the running of the ship, although many on board came to appreciate the skills such women brought with them.

Some of these women became competent navigators, a skill not usually associated with 19th-century women, but one which could be put to good use, especially if a ship was short-handed.[172] Fidelia Heard, sailing with her husband Captain John Jay Heard in 1853, describes how she learnt to find the daily position of the ship:

> *I took my first lesson in navigation this afternoon, commenced learning to box the compass… looked through the quadrant for the first time and have been studying to find the difference of*

---

170 Seaborn, R. Laurel. 'Seafaring Women: An Investigation of Material Culture for Potential Archaeological Diagnostics of Women on Nineteenth-Century Sailing Ships.' Master's thesis, East Carolina University, 2014, p.x. Accessed 7 October 2022, https://thescholarship.ecu.edu/bitstream/handle/10342/4535/Seaborn_ecu_0600O_11155.pdf?sequence=1&isAllowed=y

171 A lightweight, fast, and nimble warship.

172 Seaborn, R. Laurel. 'Seafaring Women: An Investigation of Material Culture for Potential Archaeological Diagnostics of Women on Nineteenth-Century Sailing Ships.' Master's thesis, East Carolina University, 2014, pp.4–5. Accessed 7 October 2022, https://thescholarship.ecu.edu/bitstream/handle/10342/4535/Seaborn_ecu_0600O_11155.pdf?sequence=1&isAllowed=y

latitude and longitude. Hope to be able to do it myself ere long… The Capt. Paid me a great compliment today by copying my ship's reckoning into his book.[173]

Sewing skills were also much in demand on board, and as a seamstress Jane would most likely have been able to keep both her family's and the crew's clothing in reasonable repair and have been adept at altering her own clothes to suit life aboard a ship. Clothes worn by 19th-century women were not suited for sailing. Floor-length skirts with crinolines, hoops, or bustles, tight corsets, dainty shoes, and trimmed bonnets were elegant for wearing onshore but were uncomfortable and even dangerous when coping with a rough sea and a howling wind, so on board Jane would have worn a dress made of cheap hard-wearing material that did not show the dirt, and was made, or cut down, to ankle length. This would be covered by an apron. She probably also wore a sunbonnet made of cotton which was easily washed and more practical than the decorated bonnet she might wear ashore.

Smaller ships like the *Roseau* did not have a doctor on board and it was the responsibility of the ship's captain to do what he could with the limited resources available in his medicine chest when a member of his crew or his family became sick or had an accident. Jane would have nursed any crew member who needed her attention, although her social status as the captain's wife dictated that she, along with her daughters, were generally separated from the hands. Ship's mates were an exception to the rule, as they usually ate meals with the captain and his family in the aft cabin and slept in berths off the

---

[173] Druett, Joan. *Hen Frigates: Wives of Merchant Captains Under Sail*. New York: Simon and Schuster, 1998, p.39.

aft cabin's salon.[174] Jane may also have spent time nursing Rosea, her youngest daughter, whose health was always delicate. She died from tuberculosis at the age of ten, but a break from the damp and foggy climate of London to spend time in the warm Caribbean climate surely prolonged her short life.

Jane also had the considerable responsibility of making sure her children came to no harm while they sailed to and from St Vincent. During bad weather they were kept below decks and Jane would have identified with captain's wife, Mary Rowland, who writes that in bad weather:

> *I have to keep the children in close confinement below and they are very troublesome in such times. The youngest requires constant watching to save her from broken limbs, as she has such a bad habit of climbing, regardless of the consequences.*[175]

All five of Jane's children sailed on the *Roseau* from a fairly early age and learnt basic skills while under way: her son Henry learnt to walk while on board and recalled that when he fell after an unsuccessful effort at remaining upright the deck often felt sticky because of leakage of the sugar molasses they carried from St Vincent to London.[176] As her sons grew older she would still have been able to keep an eye on them, as both were employed on the ship as cabin boys during several of their father's voyages.

Many captain's wives kept journals as they travelled, but as research has not brought to light anything written by Jane the

---

174 Ibid., p.6.
175 Druett, Joan. *Hen Frigates: Wives of Merchant Captains Under Sail*. New York: Simon and Schuster, 1998, p.100.
176 *Blewett Family: Henry Blewett 1836–1891*. Accessed 10 October 2022, http://www.mygenealogies.co.uk/Blewett/BLEW-B3.htm

following excerpts from the journal of Minerva Sears, another captain's wife who sailed the Atlantic at around the same time as Jane, gives an idea of what life on board *Roseau* might have been like:

> *This day I am suffering very much from a sick feeling and have felt this some days past… This day is very pleasant. The air is very clear and I am spending most of my time on deck as the air serves to revive me.*[177]
>
> *The steward is yet very sick… we likewise have one man forward sick with the dysentery… He is very much reduced. A ship is a very bad place to be sick in – they cannot possibly have the attention they need.*[178]
>
> *…at 9 pm was struck by a heavy sea… It was a most dreadful night for me. I didn't sleep for all night and there was much anxiety felt by all on board. That night she threw two men from her wheel and they are now laid up from the effects of the fall… I was up and dressed and looking around to see if there was any water coming in and every lurch of the ship would quite throw me off my feet.*[179]
>
> *Since dinner there has appeared a sail on the weather bow… I wish she would come along and give us some newspapers and then we could be getting the news and that would take up our minds for a short time. I am in hopes we shall see some more tomorrow as we are now on the track of vessels bound for the West Indies.*[180]

As she travelled regularly to St Vincent and spent time on the

---

177 Sears, Minerva. *Journal of the Captain's Wife: an 1852 Voyage from Calcutta to Boston;* transcribed and edited by Matthew McKnight. Diary File, 2017, [p.1].
178 Ibid., [p.6].
179 Ibid., [p.9].
180 Ibid., [p.16].

VUE DE KINGSTOWN, CAPITALE DE SAINT-VINCENT.

Jeunesse, Auguste. View of Kingstown. From: Fortunay, Dantès. Nouvelle Géographie de l'île d'Haïti: Contenant des Notions Historiques et Topographiques sur les Autres Antilles. Port-au-Prince: Fortunay, 1888.

island, Jane would have looked forward to participating in the social life of Kingstown, the capital of the island. A committed Methodist like her husband, she regularly attended the Methodist chapel, where the family were so much a part of the local community that Henry paid an annual rent on a pew so that his family could be assured of a regular seat during chapel services.[181] Methodism was well established in St Vincent, and the Kingstown Chapel, built in 1840, was an impressive building:

Commodious and elegant… it was erected at a cost of about 7000 pounds… and being furnished with galleries, will seat nearly two

---

181 Appleby, Sue. *The Cornish in the Caribbean: From the 17th to the 19th Centuries.* Kibworth Beauchamp: Matador, 2019, p.154.

thousand persons. It is generally well attended by a respectable and intelligent congregation, chiefly of black and coloured persons.[182]

She and Henry may well have made friends with Cornishman William Cocks, who arrived in Kingstown in 1876 to minister to the St Vincent Methodists, to be joined two years later by his wife-to-be, Emily Hales from the Cornish village of St Agnes. The pair married at the Kingstown Methodist Chapel in 1878, and perhaps the Blewett family attended the wedding.

Jane's visits to St Vincent became less frequent as Scruttons trade with the island faced increased competition both from other sugar-producing islands which – with a less mountainous topography than that of St Vincent, were able to produce sugar more efficiently and economically – and from the subsidised sugar beet grown in Europe. As the sugar trade on St Vincent declined, local shopkeepers and estate owners found it more difficult to make a profit, and were unable to afford the imported goods brought by the *Roseau*.

To remain profitable Scruttons began to make the change from sailing ships to steamships, and for a while Jane's husband joined the growing number of captains who, faced with unemployment, learnt new skills and signed on with a steamship, usually as a mate. Steamship owners did not encourage their captains to take family members aboard, and Jane no longer sailed with Henry. After his ship sank while at anchor in Lisbon harbour, he left the Merchant Navy and, with Jane, returned to the Mousehole fishing fleet for a few years before returning to life aboard a steamship, only to be shipwrecked off the coast of Brazil.

Life for the Blewett family was now less financially comfortable

---

[182] Moister, William. *Memorials of Missionary Labours in Western Africa and the West Indies…* 3rd ed., London: [Wesleyan Conference Office], 1850, p.324.

Trinity Green and Alms Houses. Photo by Peter Thwaite, 2009.

than during the St Vincent years. Jane lived in London with her son Charles, while her husband, now fifty-five and surely ready for retirement, found a position as a third mate on a steamer bound for India. But the steamer ran aground near Madras, and Henry, already suffering from a bad cold, joined the rest of the crew as they left the ship. Travelling in open boats they eventually reached Madras, but the journey worsened Henry's condition. Once ashore, he was immediately admitted to the Madras Hospital, but his health continued to deteriorate, and he died of pneumonia in the hospital on the last day of 1891.

After Henry's death, Jane continued to live in London, receiving a pension from the Corporation of Trinity House, which had been founded in 1695 to support retired master mariners and their widows. The corporation provided widows not only with a pension but with housing, and maintained several almshouses at

Trinity Green in Whitechapel, not far from Stepney, where Jane had spent much of her married life. Built around a tree-lined green, the houses were well designed and comfortable, and in 1907 one was made available to Jane.

Here she spent the last fourteen years of her life in pleasant surroundings, no doubt spending time with the other mariners and their widows reminiscing about her life as a sailing captain's wife and the times she had spent on the island of St Vincent. She died, at the age of eighty-three, in 1921.[183]

Elizabeth Wingfield, Eliza Jaco and Jane Wright were all born into families of the Middling Sort – although at different levels – and in various ways managed to maintain their places in contemporary society. Before her marriage Elizabeth had drawn up an agreement with her soon-to-be husband that enabled her to keep control of the capital investments she had made as a single woman, and to continue to benefit from the dividends they provided, while Eliza made a living and supported her family as a single parent through her work as a governess, and by her writing and teaching. Jane, meanwhile, managed her home and her family while her husband sailed the world, and after his death was able to access the pension and housing offered by the Corporation of Trinity House which enabled her to spend her long widowhood in relative comfort. All three women managed to control at least part of their lives through their own independent efforts.

---

183 *Wright Family: Jane Wright 1837–1921*. Accessed 10 October 2023, http://www.mygenealogies.co.uk/Wright/WRIG-B3.htm

4

'Dear Sister': Wesleyan Methodist Missionary Women

Philippa Ann West was twenty-three when she left the village of St Breock in north Cornwall and sailed out to Jamaica to marry George Savery, a young Methodist minister from Devonport in Devon, who she had most likely met while he was living in the village of Egloshayle, near to St Breock. George was accepted into the Ministry in 1838 when he was twenty-three years old and soon volunteered to serve as a foreign missionary. Leaving Philippa behind, he went out to Jamaica in 1842[184] and was appointed to minister to the community of Grateful Hill, a rural area in St Catherine's Parish, about 16 miles (26km) from the city of Kingston.[185] The Methodist Missionary Society encouraged its missionaries to marry, believing in the traditional role of a wife as a source of stability and comfort to husband and family, and the importance of providing an example of settled family life to the communities the missionaries hoped to convert and serve. Philippa

---

184 Foster, Henry Blaine. *Rise and Progress of Wesleyan-Methodism in Jamaica*. London: Wesleyan Conference Office, 1881, p.69. Accessed 3 November 2022, https://books.google.com.ag/books?id=muoCAAAAQAAJ&printsec=frontcover&source=gbs_ge_summary_r&cad=0#v=onepage&q&f=false.

185 Kingston did not become the capital of Jamaica until 1872, replacing Spanish Town.

was just one of many Methodist women who went overseas to marry a missionary she had developed a steady relationship with back at home; while other women would accompany a missionary husband to his destination. Philippa and George were married in Kingston in December 1843[186] and set up house at the Grateful Hill Methodist Mission, where there was a thriving Methodist community of about 500 who were, it was said, 'kind and peaceable Church members, [while the] climate was healthful'.[187]

Wesleyan Methodism had been introduced into the Caribbean by Nathaniel Gilbert, a wealthy planter and lawyer from Antigua who had converted to Methodism in 1759 after meeting John Wesley in London. On his return to Antigua, Gilbert began to preach to his family and to his enslaved workers, and encouraged the development of several Methodist Societies on the island. With the help of the Revd Dr Thomas Coke, one of John Wesley's most accomplished disciples, Wesleyan Methodism then spread from Antigua to the other Leeward Islands and Barbados, and reached Jamaica in 1789. Early missionaries in Jamaica focused on educating the enslaved, a policy which aroused often violent opposition from plantation owners, who believed education would contribute to unrest and rebellion among the people they owned. Although the missionaries stressed that their educational efforts would result in a more stable enslaved workforce, the planters' worst fears were realised in 1831 with the outbreak of the Sam Sharpe Rebellion, the uprising of enslaved people experienced by Anne Daniell, and which was put down with great severity.

---

186 Information about Philippa's marriage from Chris Sweeney, in an email of 2 November 2022.

187 Findlay, G.G. and W.W. Holdsworth. *The History of the Wesleyan Methodist Missionary Society*. Vol.2. London: Epworth Press, 1921, p.118. Accessed 3 November 2011, https://ia800205.us.archive.org/17/items/historyofwesleya02finduoft/historyofwesleya02finduoft.pdf.

It was some years after the rebellion when Philippa arrived on Jamaica, by which time the enslaved workers, who had finally won their freedom in 1838,[188] were beginning the challenging task of making a new life for themselves. The Grateful Hill community included many recently freed men and women, and the local Mission was well established to assist in their development. A Methodist chapel had been built back in 1819 and a minister stationed there for the first time in the same year; there were two active societies, one at Grateful Hill and the other at nearby Unity, both of which had a day school for the local children.

The Wesleyan Mission Premises, Grateful Hill, Jamaica. About 1840. Courtesy of the Caroline Simpson Collection, Museum of History NSW, Australia.

---

188 Although Great Britain had passed the Emancipation Act in 1833, and it had been brought into effect in 1834, the enslaved were then 'apprenticed' to their masters in all the British possessions in the Caribbean except for Antigua, as the colonial administration considered that the enslaved were not 'ready' for freedom.

As soon as Philippa settled into her home at Grateful Hill, she would have begun to contribute to the work of the Mission. It was her responsibility to run the Mission House, receive visitors, and undertake some of her husband's responsibilities if he was unwell or visiting a distant community. She was also expected to provide her husband with children – and no matter how basic the local health care, missionary wives usually gave birth to several children while overseas. Philippa was no exception. In Jamaica she gave birth to the first three of her ten children: Ellen Mary, Ann West, and George Mearns. The Wesleyan Missionary Society hoped that such children, having been brought up within a Wesleyan missionary family, would have already learnt the skills necessary to become successful Wesleyan missionaries or missionary wives, and would help fill the ever-growing need for committed Wesleyan men and women with a vocation to minister both at home and overseas. The early education of the family's children was also largely the responsibility of the missionary wife, who, whether trained as a teacher or not, would have done the best she could with the help of whatever teaching texts were available.

There might also have been an opportunity for Philippa to play an active part in her husband's work, leading regular class meetings, or special events such as Missionary Sundays or Sunday School Anniversaries. During his life John Wesley had promoted a recognition of at least some level of spiritual equality between men and women, telling Society members to think of themselves as brothers and sisters in Christ, and encouraging the 'dear sisters' to participate fully in missionary work, by – even if reluctantly – allowing them to preach. After Wesley's death, however, the Wesleyan Methodist Society hardened its views against women preachers. From then on, only ordained preachers were appointed missionaries and, as women were ineligible for ordination because they were not officially allowed to preach, then no matter how much of a vocation a woman had for missionary work she was prevented from following the path she had chosen.[189]

This situation began to change in 1858 when the Ladies' Committee for the Amelioration of the Condition of Women in Heathen Countries, Female Education etc. was formed as an auxiliary movement within the Wesleyan Methodist Missionary Society. The Committee's objective was to train, equip, and finance the sending of woman missionaries overseas.[190] However – so as not to offend the sensibilities of those who believed a woman incapable of taking the responsibility of mission work independent of male guidance and supervision – these women were officially known as agents, not missionaries.

Although a missionary wife was not officially allowed to preach, there were other ways she could contribute to the development of the local community. Some wives had teaching skills – whether professional or not – and taught in the Methodist Day Schools where, although they taught under the general guidance of the Methodist curriculum, they had an opportunity to work independently. Others were experienced – if not qualified – nurses. Wives could also often interact with local women more easily than could their husbands, and were able to share the Methodist message both within organised groups and more informally as they visited the sick, the elderly and the destitute.

The fundamental tenet of Methodism is that all are equal in the

---

[189] Information provided by John Lenton, Hon. Librarian, Wesley Historical Society Library, in email message of 22 April 2021.
[190] *Dictionary of Methodism in Britain and Ireland: Women's Work*. Accessed 16 December 2022, https://dmbi.online/index.php?do=app.entry&id=3054.

sight of God – but, however much missionary wives believed in this religious equality, when it came to *social* equality it was quite another matter. Like other women of their time, they were products of a class-conscious Victorian society, and as O'Callaghan notes, this ingrained class consciousness negatively affected their ability to minister to the local community as it inevitably 'foregrounds the ambivalent nature of the white woman's empowerment through ministering to those who, however "saved", could never be equals'.[191]

In turn, members of the plantocracy considered themselves superior to the non-conformist missionaries. Unlike the clergy and their wives and families sent out by the Anglican Church, who were usually from wealthy landowning and often aristocratic families, the non-conformist missionaries – including Methodists, Baptists, and Moravians – were mostly of the Middling Sort. They were not seen as the social equals of the élites of colonial society, and it would be unlikely for a planter's family to consider inviting a missionary family to their residence for a social visit. The non-conformist missionary family, then, as Zacek and Brown write, 'occupied an awkward and difficult position in nineteenth-century Caribbean society'.[192]

Nevertheless, despite this 'awkward and difficult position' non-conformist missionary families strove to be seen as respectable members of society, and the importance of respectability was in turn central to the non-conformist missionaries' efforts to educate the members of the communities to whom they ministered.[193] If

---

191 O'Callaghan, Evelyn. *Women Writing the West Indies, 1804–1939: 'A Hot Place, Belonging to Us'.* London: Routledge, 2004, p.99–100.

192 Zacek, Natalie and Laurence Brown. 'Unsettled Houses: The Material Culture of the Missionary Project in Jamaica in the Era of Emancipation.' *Slavery and Abolition,* p.495 (Vol.35, No.3, 2014).

193 Olwig, Karen Fog. 'The Struggle for Respectability: Methodism and Afro-Caribbean

they wanted to work effectively with local communities, missionary families could not, they believed, behave like members of the labouring classes. As the Baptist Minister Walter Dendy wrote in the 1840s, it was most inappropriate for missionaries to 'dig the ground, [while] their wives stand at the wash tub, or, cook their provisions for their respective meals'.[194]

The presentation of yourself and your family in good quality but modest clothing was seen as part of this striving for middle-class respectability: the women wore plain dresses of pale-coloured muslin and cotton, while they dressed their husbands in dark suits with no ornamentation. Along with suitable attire went the need for a well but not opulently furnished house. In the early days of Wesleyan Mission work in the Caribbean the missionary house was often modest – indeed the first residence at Grateful Hill, was a 'small wooden house-cum-chapel'[195] which the then minister fully expected to collapse during the earthquake that shook the area in 1824. Later residences were more substantial and well built, with furnishings which, although they reflected the values of thrift, sobriety, and simplicity expected of non-Conformist families, were of good quality – although without any unnecessary additions such as the frills and tassels beloved by many Victorian homeowners.

Given the large size of many mission districts and the difficulties of travelling long distances over mountainous terrain in many of the colonies, missionary families needed some form of transport if they were to communicate effectively with local communities. Given the long distances and the terrain, walking was certainly not an option and,

---

Culture on Nineteenth Century Nevis'. *Nieuwe West-Indische Gids/New West Indian Guide*. (Vol.64, Nos.3 and 4, 1990), p.93.
194 Ibid., p.497.
195 Ibid., p.498.

while a saddle horse was the most useful in rural areas, a horse and carriage was more appropriate in town. As Walter Dendy writes again:

> [To] attempt to claim respectability and prestige as a 'walk-foot buccra' [white person walking] was to be ridiculed by black and white West Indian alike, and many mission stations in Jamaica maintained two-horse chaises, despite the complaints of the London authorities that this represented a needless expense, as missionaries in Britain were accustomed to walking whenever possible.[196]

Employing numbers of servants was another marker of importance and respectability, and even though the Methodist Missionary Society was of the view that one servant per family was quite enough, overseas missionary wives were usually assisted by numerous cooks, maids, and gardeners as they went about their daily lives. Being mostly of the Middling Sort, many women were unfamiliar with managing large numbers of servants and found this level of domestic assistance a challenge.

After ministering to the Grateful Hill community for some years, the Methodist Missionary Society expanded Philippa's husband's responsibilities to include nearby Stoney Hill, and, as he spent more time away from the family home, Philippa's workload increased, as in addition to raising her children and managing the mission house she now most likely had to undertake some of George's activities at Grateful Hill while he ministered to the Stoney Hill community.

The family stayed in Jamaica until 1850, when they returned to Cornwall before moving on to Dorset and Berkshire, as George was

---

196 Ibid., p.497.

appointed to various ministries throughout England before retiring to Oxford, where he died in 1885. After his death Philippa went to live with her youngest son and daughter, Samuel Servington and Edith Mary, who lived in Bilton, a village near Harrogate in Yorkshire. Here Philippa died in 1891 at the age of seventy-one.

The elder of Philippa's two daughters born in Jamaica, Ellen Mary (1845–1930), married London-born William Cocks, a draper who came from a Cornish family. The couple settled in London and had four children, two girls and two boys. Following her husband's death in 1921, Ellen remained in London, dying in 1930 at the age of eighty-five. Her sister, Anne West (1846–1926), the younger of Philippa's Jamaica-born daughters, fulfilled the Methodist Missionary Society's hope that missionary children would provide a ready source of committed men and women ready to swell the ranks of those ministering both at home and abroad. She married Albert Bishop, a Wesleyan Methodist minister, and like her mother Philippa travelled with her husband throughout England, giving birth to four daughters and two sons along the way. Anne died in 1926 at the age of seventy-nine.[197]

As Wesleyan Methodism spread around the Caribbean during the 19th century the Methodist Missionary Society sent increasing numbers of missionaries to the region and, given the popularity of Methodism in Cornwall, among these new missionaries were many Cornish men with Cornish wives. One was Mary Thomas (1823–1892) who had been born in Redruth in the centre of Cornwall's mining district and had married Cornish Wesleyan Minister Samuel Annear (1819–1886) in St Austell in 1843. She was the daughter of an ironmonger, he the son of a carpenter.[198] Soon after her marriage

---

197 Information provided by Chris Sweeney, in an email of 3 November 2022.
198 Information provided by John Heath, Online Parish Clerk (Genealogy) for Redruth,

she accompanied Samuel to West Africa, where he was appointed to minister in an area then known as the Gold Coast,[199] but in 1848 she went to live in a quite different part of the world – the Bahamas. Samuel was appointed to the Mission in Nassau, the capital of the Bahamas, on the island of New Providence, a posting which also gave him the responsibility of ministering to the community on the island of Abaco and its surrounding islands and cays. Abaco, also known as Great Abaco, lies about 55 miles (90km) north of Nassau and is the largest island of the Abaco group, which stretches for some 120 miles (193km) in the northern Bahamas.

Once she arrived in the Bahamas Mary had to adapt to life on a small island – quite a change from the sprawling coast of West Africa

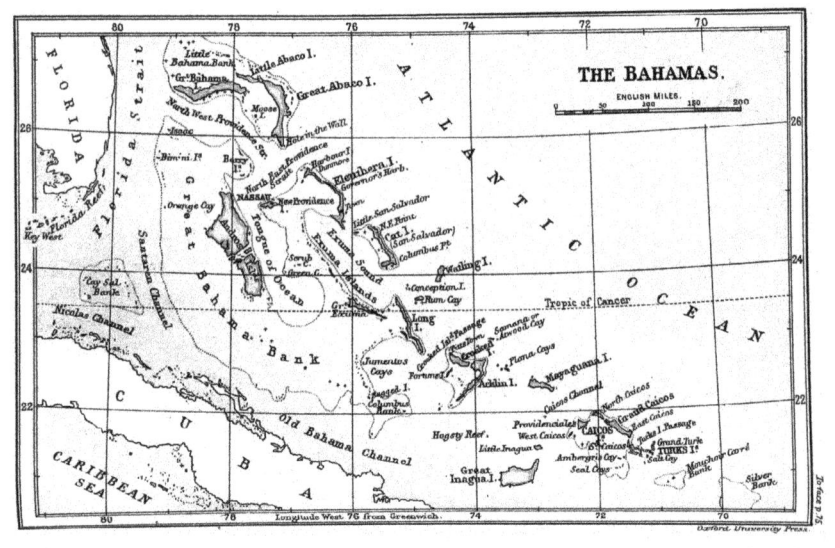

A Map of the Islands of the Bahamas. From: Lucas, C. P. Historical Geography of the British Colonies. Vol 2. Oxford: Clarendon Press, 1888, p.96.

Mawnan, Mawgan in Meneage, and St Martin in Meneage, Cornwall, in an email message of 10 November 2022.

199 Now Ghana.

– and to Wesleyan Methodist communities which operated differently from those she had been a part of on the Gold Coast. In most of the Caribbean, Wesleyan Methodism had developed under the guidance of British missionaries sent by the London-based Wesleyan Methodist Missionary Society, but in the Bahamas the early missionaries were sent from the newly founded United States by the Primitive Methodist Connection. This breakaway church had been established in Charleston, North Carolina, in 1794, when its members had split from the established United States Methodist Church after failing to resolve a number of differences of opinion concerning the running of the Church. The Bahamas archipelago was a natural focus for the Primitive Methodists as they began their missionary work, as the Wesleyan Methodists had not yet sent any missionaries there, and the islands lay close to the coast of North Carolina, where the Primitive Methodists were based.[200] However, the early Primitive Methodist Connection missionaries sent to the Bahamas unfortunately proved ill-suited to their chosen vocation: the first was imprisoned for beating his wife, and two men sent out later were reported to have fallen 'into disgraceful sin'.[201] Lacking stable leadership, the local Methodist community struggled to continue, and asked the Methodist Missionary Society to send them a missionary from London. One was sent in 1799,[202] and by the time Mary and her husband arrived in the Bahamas a stable if small Methodist community had been established. It was a society which, due to its foundation under the guidance of the Primitive Methodist Connection 'developed an independent Methodism rooted in its experience'.[203]

---

[200] Bundy, David. 'The African and Caribbean Origins of Methodism in the Bahamas.' *Methodist History*, p.175. (Vol.53, No.3, April 2015).

[201] Ibid., p.176.

[202] Ibid., p.177.

[203] Ibid., p.183.

If Mary found the behaviour of the Bahamian Methodist community in some ways a challenge to her Wesleyan Methodist beliefs, there was one local activity with which she, like John James, the estate manager on Barbuda, was very familiar. As in Cornwall, the salvaging of ships that ran aground on the many reefs or were wrecked in the shallow waters off the low-lying islands of the Bahamas was common practice, and the proceeds, although not always declared to the government officials, made just as important a contribution to the local economy of the Bahamas as they did to the economy of Cornwall.

While Mary no doubt found the island of Abaco rather remote and the living conditions basic, she nevertheless gave birth to her first child, Mary Ann, at the Mission there, in 1848. Then in 1850 her second child, Emma, was born, this time at the Nassau Mission. In contrast to the Mission at Abaco, it was housed in a pleasantly proportioned building which provided comfortable living quarters,

The Wesleyan Chapel and Mission Premises, Nassau, in the Eastern District of New Providence, Bahamas, 1849.

more frequent opportunities for socialising, and better access to whatever health services were available.

The Annear family left the Bahamas in 1851, bound for England via Philadelphia, and over the next few years Mary gave birth to four more children: three boys and one girl. By 1861 Mary was living with her children in a small town house in Union Place, Truro,[204] while her husband continued to travel the world to spread the Wesleyan Methodist word, both as a missionary and as a public speaker. During the 1870s and 1880s he travelled frequently to the United States and Canada, where he delivered a series of lectures on the dangers of alcohol. He died in Canada in 1886.[205]

By 1891 Mary had moved to the village of Kinson in Dorset, where she lived with her daughter, Abaco-born Mary Ann, now Mary Ann Skeats, and where she died a year later.[206] Mary is buried with her husband Samuel in West Norwood Cemetery, one of seven private cemeteries founded on the outskirts of London in the 19th century, which were popular final places of rest for the wealthy and the well known. Here, Mary and Samuel keep company with such famous names as Isabella Beeton, author of *Beeton's Book of Household Management*, and Henry Tate, who made his money by establishing a sugar company, today known as Tate & Lyle, and established the

---

204 The National Archives of the UK. Public Record Office. *Census Returns of England and Wales, 1861*. Mary Annear. Class: RG 9; Piece: 1558; Folio: 49; Page: 23; GSU roll: 542831.

205 Friends of the West Norwood Cemetery. *Lives of the Dead: A Self-Guided Walk Round West Norwood Cemetery*. London: Royal Geographical Society, 2014, p.39. Accessed 7 November 2022, https://www.discoveringbritain.org/content/discoveringbritain/walk%20booklets/West%20Norwood%20DB%20walk%20-%20written%20guide.pdf.

206 The National Archives of the UK. Public Record Office. *Census Returns of England and Wales, 1891*. Mary A. Skeats. Class: RG12; Piece: 1637; Folio: 149; Page: 43; GSU roll: 6096747.

Tate Gallery. Why a Cornish Methodist couple – both partners from families who belonged more to the working class than to the Middling Sort – should choose to be buried at the élite and private West Norwood Cemetery is unclear, but they were perhaps a couple who, as dedicated non-conformist missionaries, became well respected, and rose in the stratified Victorian society of their day.

Like Philippa Ann West, Elizabeth Ann Williams (1855?) left her home in Cornwall and travelled out to the Caribbean to meet her husband-to-be, John Kernick (1853–1921). John had been born in Crantock, a village near Newquay on the north coast of Cornwall, not far from the hamlet of Penwinnick, where Elizabeth – often known as Lizzie – was living. Elizabeth's father was a farmer from the village of Stoke Climsland in the Tamar Valley, while her mother was from Poplar in the East End of London, where Elizabeth and two of her sisters were born. After entering the Ministry in 1875 John Kernick

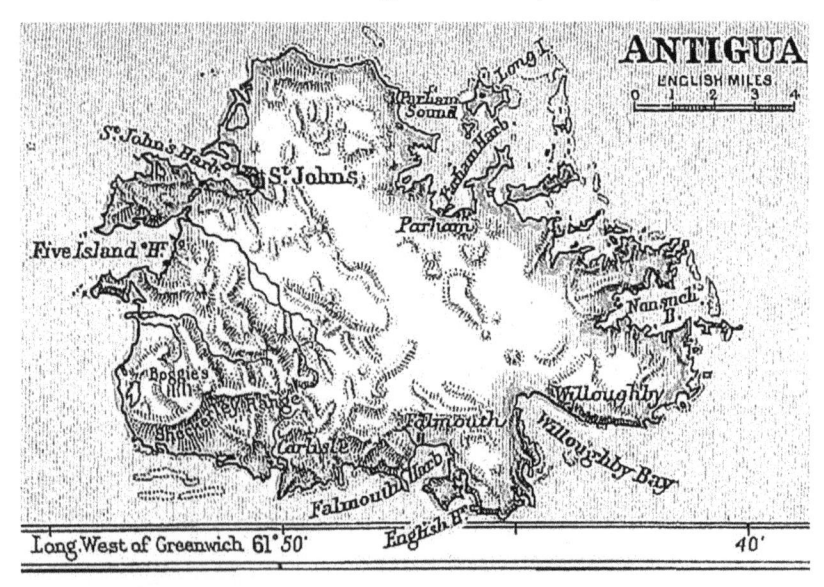

A Map of the Island of Antigua. From: Lucas, C. P. Historical Geography of the British Colonies. Vol 2. Oxford: Clarendon Press, 1888, p.158.

Southeast View of the Ebenezer Methodist Chapel, St John's, Antigua. About 1815. Courtesy of the Caroline Simpson Collection, Museums of History NSW, Australia.

was appointed to the island of Nevis before being transferred to Antigua in 1879.

Elizabeth arrived on Antigua in September of that year, and married John a month later in the Ebenezer Methodist Chapel, a large and substantial building constructed in 1815 in St John's, Antigua's capital, at a cost of nearly £2,000.[207]

While Elizabeth was living in Antigua she gave birth to one child, a son, Frederick Walwyn, born in 1882. With only one child to look after, she had more time than many missionary wives to work with her husband as he ministered to the Antigua Wesleyan Methodist community. There were no Wesleyan Methodist women ministers at this time – women were not ordained as ministers in

---

207 Appleby, Sue. *The Cornish in the Caribbean: From the 17th to the 19th Centuries.* Kibworth Beauchamp: Matador, 2019, pp.192, 202.

the Wesleyan Methodist Church until 1974[208] [209] but, in the census of 1911 Elizabeth's occupation is recorded as 'Wesleyan Minister', albeit only by a series of ditto marks under husband John's entry.[210] This is either a mistake by the enumerator, or the result of her signifying that her commitment to Methodism was as great as her husband's and that as far as she was concerned she worked with him as an equal. The Kernick family did not spend long in the Caribbean, however, as after John had suffered a serious accident they returned to England in 1882.[211] After he had recovered his health, he was appointed to various circuits throughout the country, and Elizabeth travelled with him, giving birth to a daughter, Marion Grace, while they were living in the village of Harrington on the coast of Cumbria, and to a son, Henry Williams, in Bodmin, Cornwall.

A year after Elizabeth Williams had sailed out to Antigua, Annie Whitburn (1855–1924) left Devoran, a village near Falmouth, to marry Thomas Henry Bailey (1851–1917) on the island of St Christopher. Annie was the only daughter of Henry Whitburn, a captain in the Merchant Marine, and if – like Henry Blewett's wife Jane – she was no stranger to long sea voyages she would have taken the voyage to St Christopher in her stride. Her husband-to-be, Thomas Bailey, had been born in Gwennap, near to Gwennap Pit, where John Wesley often preached, and after entering the Ministry in 1876 he had been appointed to the island of St Barthélemy – part

---

208 *Dictionary of Methodism in Britain and Ireland: Women*. Accessed 18 November 2022, https://dmbi.online/index.php?do=app.entry&id=3051

209 Information provided by Rev. Jenny Dyer, Superintendent, Stoke-on-Trent North Methodist Circuit, in email message of 11 April 2021.

210 The National Archives of the UK. Public Record Office. *Census Returns of England and Wales, 1911*. Elizabeth Ann Kernick. RG 14; Piece: 16540; Page: 132.

211 Information provided by John Lenton, Hon. Librarian, Wesley Historical Society Library, in email message of 22 April 2021.

of the St Christopher District and commonly known as St Bart's – before transferring to Sandy Point, a town on the northwest coast of St Christopher, in 1879. Sandy Point had a well-established Wesleyan Methodist community who worshipped in a sizeable stone-built chapel built in 1830 at Crab Hill, Sandy Point. Here, Annie married Thomas in July 1880.[212]

Although based on St Christopher, Thomas also ministered to communities on the neighbouring islands of Anguilla and St Martin, which were part of the St Christopher District, so Annie became used to managing the Sandy Point Mission in his absence and looking after their daughter, Ellen Annie (1882–1952), who was born two years after her marriage. In 1883 the family moved to the island of Montserrat, part of the Antigua District, and here Thomas became Superintendent of the Montserrat Wesleyan Methodist missionaries. Unlike most of the Leeward Islands, Montserrat's population included many Roman Catholics, descended both from early Irish settlers and from men deported from England after the failed Monmouth Rebellion, and there was fierce competition for the souls of Montserratians between the Roman Catholic priests, the Anglican vicars, and the non-conformist ministers. As he reported to the Methodist Missionary Society, Thomas Bailey found this competition stressful, and it created challenges for him as he strove to increase the number of Wesleyan Methodist converts among the community.[213]

His wife undoubtedly shared his concerns but, having given birth to Ellen in 1882 and to three sons over the next four years – Thomas

---

212 Appleby, Sue. *The Cornish in the Caribbean: From the 17th to the 19th Centuries.* Kibworth Beauchamp: Matador, 2019, pp.199–200.

213 Findlay, G.G. and W.W. Holdsworth. *The History of the Wesleyan Methodist Missionary Society.* Vol.2. London: Epworth Press, 1921, p.424. Accessed 3 November 2011, https://ia800205.us.archive.org/17/items/historyofwesleya02finduoft/historyofwesleya02finduoft.pdf.

in 1883, Reginald in 1885 and Ernest a year later – she had little time to contribute to her husband's efforts to gain converts other than providing him with a nurturing and comforting environment, in line with the traditional domestic skills expected of a missionary wife. The Baileys moved back to Cornwall in 1887, where Thomas served on the Bodmin Circuit before being appointed to other circuits in Leicestershire, Derbyshire, Cheshire, Yorkshire, and Lancashire. As she accompanied her husband on his travels Annie gave birth to three more children: William, Herbert, and Edith. She outlived her husband by seven years, dying in 1924 at the age of sixty-nine.

Annie's St Christopher-born daughter Ellen married Herbert Pearce, an electrical engineer, in Sheffield in 1909 and gave birth to one son, Kenneth Maxwell. In 1920 she found employment in the West Sussex port town of Newhaven, working with the local police force as an 'aliens attendant', looking after female immigrants. This employment opportunity had come about following the introduction of the 1920 Aliens Order, designed to limit immigration to England after the widespread unemployment and social unrest following the First World War had led to mass emigration from Eastern and Central Europe. The order introduced the requirement for immigrants to be medically inspected before landing at a time when an understanding of the personal, local, national, and international public health issues involved in causing and preventing infectious diseases was just developing.[214] Then, as now, immigrant groups from overseas were often seen as more likely to carry infectious diseases and therefore be less desirable as potential citizens. Did Ellen's early childhood among Caribbean people and experience of different cultures give her at least

---

214 Taylor, Becky. 'Immigration, Statecraft and Public Health: The 1920 Aliens Order, Medical Examinations and the Limitations of the State in England.' *Social History of Medicine*, pp.512–533 (Vol.29, No.3, 2016).

some understanding of, and sympathy for, the immigrant women with whom she worked? It is to be hoped that it did. She and her husband later retired to Cheshire, where she died in 1952, aged sixty-nine.

During her residence on St Christopher, Annie Whitburn would have known William Lanyon Bennett (1856–1936) who ministered to the people of the island alongside her husband between 1880 and 1882. William had been born in Gwithian, a village on the north coast of Cornwall, and had gone to St Christopher in 1880 to minister for two years to the community in Basseterre, the capital of the island, before being transferred to Antigua. Soon after his arrival on that island he was joined by his future wife, Clara Morley James (1856–1943), who had been born in Camborne, a mining town some 5 miles (8km) from Gwithian. As the *Saint Christopher Advertiser and Weekly Intelligencer* reported, they married in the Wesleyan Chapel in St John's, Antigua, in May 1883:

> *The Revd. William Lanyon Bennett, late Wesleyan Minister in the island, was, on Thursday the 3rd instant, married in the Wesleyan Chapel of St John's, Antigua by the Revd. J.H. Darrell, assisted by the Revd. R. Rossell [sic], to Miss Clara Morley James, of Camborne, Cornwall, England.*[215]

In 1884, Clara and her husband were transferred to the island of Dominica which, along with Montserrat, was part of the Antigua Circuit. Here Clara gave birth to her first child, a daughter who was named Kate Lanyon (1884–1941). William was known as a 'good pastor and a faithful friend',[216] and Clara, as a dutiful wife, would

---

215 'The Revd. William Lanyon Bennett ...' *Saint Christopher Advertiser and Weekly Intelligencer.* P.4. (Tuesday 15 May 1883). James Darrell and Richard Rossall were fellow Wesleyan ministers.
216 Bennett, Dennis Stanley Lanyon. *William Lanyon Bennett, Born 1856: His Life Story.*

have supported her husband's efforts. Like fellow missionary wife Agnes Satchell, who was living on Dominica at around the same time as Clara, she could also have taken advantage of the relative physical freedom that living in the Caribbean offered some missionary wives. Mrs Satchell clearly relished this freedom, writing in her memoir, *Reminiscences of a Missionary Life in the Caribbean*, of the enjoyment she took in riding horses, climbing mountains on foot, and travelling by boat along Dominica's fast-flowing rivers as she visited the various island communities – activities she would most likely not have been able to pursue as a minister's wife in England.[217]

By 1866 the Bennett family was back in Cornwall. Many Cornish Wesleyan ministers were appointed to circuits throughout Britain when they returned from missionary service overseas, but William spent much of his remaining working life among the Cornish communities he knew best, and in Cornwall Clara gave birth to four more children – Emma Morley, Richard Stanley, Ellen Burrall, and Vivian Edmonds. In later life Clara and William lived in a house in Wadebridge, a town in north Cornwall near to Padstow and, perhaps because the family had happy memories of their time on St Christopher – which is often known as St Kitts – the house was named St Kitts. Following William's death in 1936, Clara and her Dominican-born daughter Kate continued to live in Wadebridge. Kate never married, and died at the house in Wadebridge in 1941. Her mother Clara died five years later, and all three – husband William, wife Clara, and daughter Kate – are buried in the churchyard of St Breock.

Clara, like the other women who have so far featured in this

Unpublished notes, 1982. Used with permission of George Waterman, via email message of 16 June 2016.
217 O'Callaghan, Evelyn. *Women Writing the West Indies, 1804–1939: 'A Hot Place, Belonging to Us'*. London: Routledge, 2004, p.99.

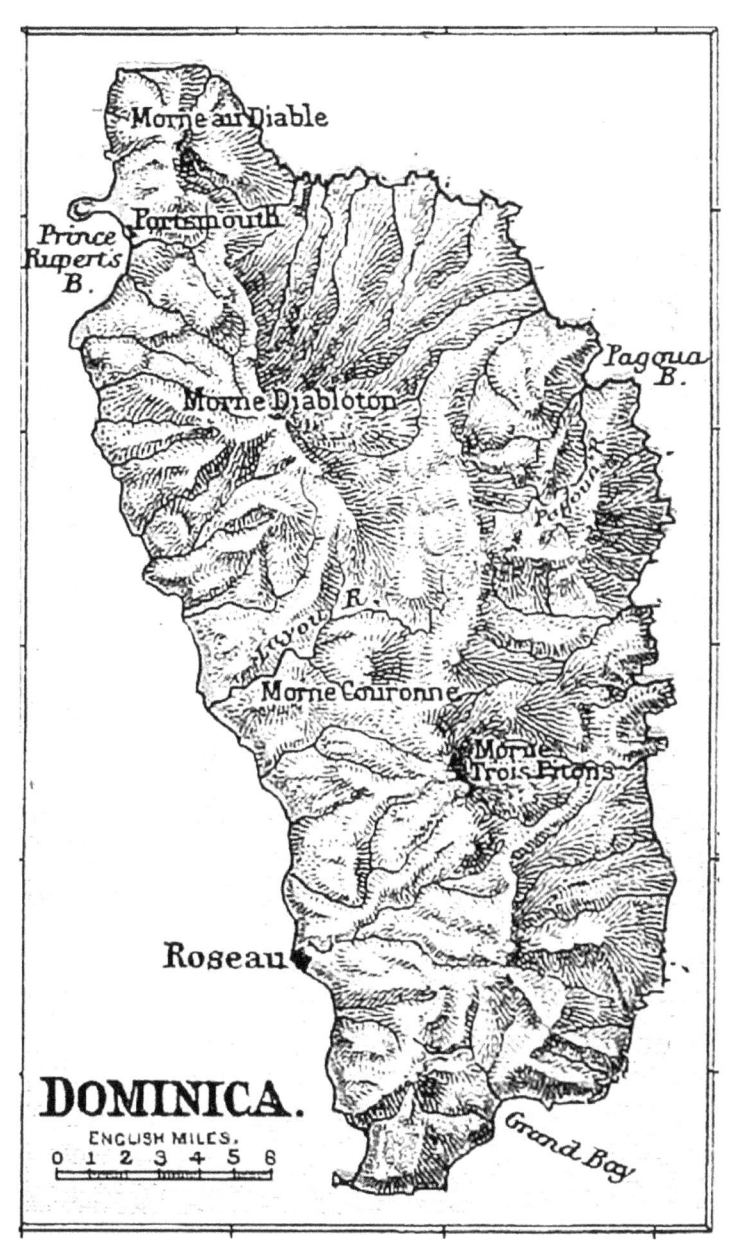

A Map of the Island of Dominica. From: Lucas, C. P. Historical Geography of the British Colonies. *Vol 2. Oxford: Clarendon Press, 1888, p.158.*

chapter, married a man who managed to survive the continuous threat of death from yellow fever, malaria, or one of the other tropical diseases that put an end to the vocations of many missionaries in the Caribbean. Emily Hales (1856?) was, however, not so fortunate. Born in Gwennap, in 1878 she left her father's farm in St Agnes to join her future husband, William Francis Cocks (1856–1881) on the island of St Vincent, where he had been appointed to minister to the local Methodist community in 1876.[218] On 22 November 1878 the couple were married in the Kingstown Methodist Chapel in Kingstown, afterwards moving into the Methodist Missionary Residence situated next door to the Chapel.[219]

Here their first child was born, and here Emily might well have entertained fellow Methodists Captain William Blewett, his wife Jane, and their children, as the Cocks were living in Kingstown

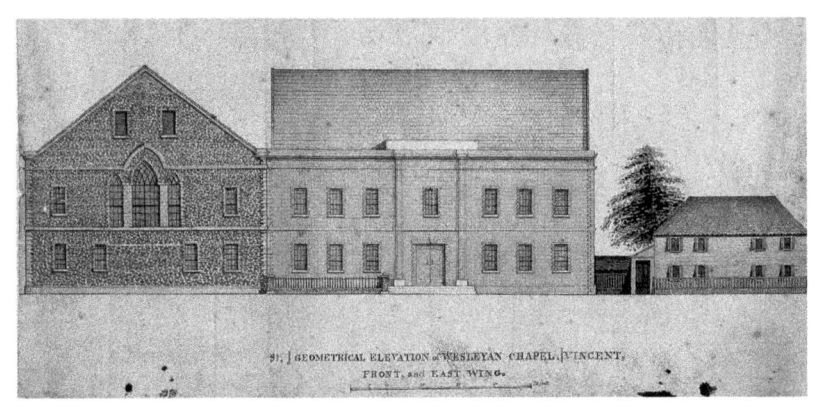

Geometrical Elevation of the Wesleyan Chapel [Kingstown], St Vincent. Left to Right: The Front, The East Wing and The Missionary's Residence. Courtesy of the Caroline Simpson Collection, Museums of History NSW, Australia.

---

218 Courtney Library. *Cornish People Overseas from 1840: Index Compiled from Local Newspapers*. Truro: Courtney Library, nd.
219 Ibid.

during the period when Captain Blewett made frequent voyages to the island on the *Roseau*.

In 1880 William Cocks was transferred to Bridgetown, Barbados, and there in 1881 Emily gave birth to a second child – John Edgar Wright. Unfortunately for the Cocks family, yellow fever was rampant on the island in that year and in July 1881 both William and her firstborn died from the disease.[220] A missionary widow did not always choose to leave her overseas posting and cease missionary work after the death of her husband (Wesleyan Methodist missionary wife Mrs Gordon, for example, stayed on independently as a teacher in St Christopher for ten years after the death of her husband, before going to teach in Sierra Leone in 1845, and eventually remarrying[221]), but after William's death, Emily decided to return to Cornwall with her baby son John. Once back home she was able to rebuild her life; in 1886 she married Cumberland-born Joseph Hall in Truro, who adopted John, and she moved with her new family to Holyhead on Holy Island, adjacent to Anglesey in Wales. Here, Emily gave birth to two daughters, Irene Theodora and Dorothy Greta, and a son, Joseph Spencer.[222] Now settled in Holyhead, Emily had no further involvement in the world of Wesleyan Methodist missionaries, and most likely would have wanted to put her Caribbean experience, which had cost her the lives of her husband and firstborn child, behind her.

For a 19th-century woman who, unlike Emily, did want to devote her life to the Wesleyan Methodist cause overseas, her only course of

---

220 'Letters from Barbados'. *The Royal Gazette: Bermuda Commercial and General Advertiser and Recorder*, p.1. (Vol.57, 23 August 1881).

221 Pritchard, John. *Methodist Women Abroad: Roles and Relationships*, p.4. Accessed 25 April 2021, methodistheritage.org.uk/missionary-history-pritchard-methodist-women-abrod02011.pdf.

222 Information supplied by Michelle Myburgh in a message dated 13 December 2022.

action before 1858 – the year when Wesleyan women formed their own organisation and began sending single women overseas – was to marry a missionary and accompany him to his appointed destination. This gave her the opportunity to assist her husband as he ministered to the local Wesleyan Methodist communities and sometimes to work independently to spread the Word as she taught in the Mission Day School, nursed the sick, or visited the elderly. Joining the missionary cause also meant giving up a settled existence in an environment she knew for a peripatetic life, moving from one Mission to another every few years, leaving newfound friends and acquaintances behind, taking responsibility for the education of her children, being left to run the Mission during her husband's frequent absences as he ministered to distant communities, and living with the knowledge that her life and that of her husband and family might suddenly be cut short by any of the tropical diseases which were endemic to the area. Whether she chose to be a 'missionary wife', taking advantage of whatever opportunities for independence presented themselves during service overseas, or a 'missionary's wife', who did as her husband and society expected of her, she had many challenges to face.

5

Mining Women

The history of mining in Cornwall is long, stretching back as far as the Bronze Age, when humans first began to mine the surface of the land for tin, and by the 18th century the mining of copper and tin – along with smaller quantities of arsenic, silver, zinc, and lead – had grown to be Cornwall's major industry, the driving force of the economy, along with fishing and, to a lesser extent, agriculture. Mining was an industry in which women and girls played a major part. They were known as bal maidens,[223] and it was in the early 1700s that they were first employed on a commercial basis to dress the ore sent to the surface of the mines. There are no figures for the number of mine workers employed at the time,[224] but in 1827 a detailed estimate of the numbers of men and women working in the Cornish mining industry was published.[225] These estimates, with the addition of an estimate of the percentage of women employed in the mines, are reproduced in Table 1.

---

223 'Bal' is the Cornish word for 'a mining place'.
224 Mayers, Lynne. *Balmaidens*. Penzance: Hypatia Press, 2004, p.15.
225 Leifchild, J.R. *Cornwall: Its Mines and Miners; With Sketches of Scenery*. 2nd Ed. London: Longman, Brown Green, 1857, p.172.

Table 1: *The Number of Men and Women, and Percentage of Women, Working in the Cornish Mining Industry in 1827.*

Type of mine	Men	Women	% of Women
Copper	11,639	2,098	17.98%
Tin	5,706	130	2.28%
Lead	419	21	4.27%
Minerals not specified	533	27	5.06%

As these figures show, at that time a significant number of women were employed in a variety of mineral mines, with the largest number by far – almost 18 per cent of the total workforce – employed in the copper mines.

During the 18th and for much of the first half of the 19th century, the Cornish mining industry thrived, but the exploitation of overseas sources of copper, which could be mined more cheaply, was already under way, and Cornish miners, renowned for their hard rock mining skills, were not slow to seek employment with newly established foreign mining enterprises that offered better wages for their specialised skills and experience than did local mines.[226] The production of Cornish copper peaked in the 1850s, but after the banking crisis of 1866 the price fell drastically and production declined. Tin production continued to grow, peaking in the 1870s, but recurring low metal prices caused even tin production to falter, and by the 1890s Cornish mining was in general decline.

One of the overseas copper mines which attracted Cornish miners in the 1830s was on the south-eastern tip of the small island of Virgin Gorda in the British Virgin Islands – an area now known

---

226 Deacon, Bernard. *Cornish Mining: A Short History*. Accessed 10 July 2023, https://bernarddeacon.com/mining/cornish-mining-a-short-history/

as Coppermine Point. Copper had first been mined here by the island's Amerindian inhabitants, and in 1493 when Christopher Columbus anchored off the point he noticed the copper staining the low cliffs facing the sea and recognised it as the outcrop of a copper lode. He reported his observations to the Spanish colonial authorities and the area was subsequently mined by early Spanish colonisers. Later, sometime during the 18th century, another group of miners, possibly Dutch, briefly established a mine there.[227] A new attempt to develop and mine the area began in the mid-1830s, when the Virgin Gorda Mining Company, a syndicate of English investors, cleared the land and surveyed the old mine workings. In 1838 a shaft was sunk which revealed considerable quantities of copper ore and, with the prospects for operating the mine at a profit looking promising, the investors decided to send their resident mine agent to England 'for the purpose of procuring a few English miners, a steam engine and other necessary apparatus.'[228] Given Cornwall's reputation as a source of skilled hard rock miners the 'English' miners were, unsurprisingly, Cornish; thirty-one men sailed for Virgin Gorda, and five of them brought their wives and families with them.[229]

The miners came from the St Austell area of Cornwall, where the local economy had long depended on the extraction of tin, copper, and china clay, and where women – as shown in Table 2 – made up a substantial part of the mining workforce. The largest and most successful mines operating around the time the Cornish miners left

---

[227] Birchall, Frank and Margaret Birchall. 'The Virgin Gorda Copper Mine, British Virgin Islands', p.23. *Journal of the Trevithick Society* (No.20, 1993).

[228] Burt, R. 'Virgin Gorda Copper Mine 1839–1862'. *Industrial Archaeology Review*, p.56 (Vol.6 Issue 1, 1981).

[229] Birchall, Frank and Margaret Birchall. 'The Virgin Gorda Copper Mine, British Virgin Islands', p.23. *Journal of the Trevithick Society* (No.20, 1993).

Map of the British Virgin Islands showing Virgin Gorda at top right.

for Virgin Gorda were Fowey Consols,[230] Charlestown Mines, Par Consols, and East Crinnis Mine. These were all copper mines, and between them employed several hundred women.[231]

Table 2: *The Number of Women Working at the Larger Mines of the St Austell Area in 1836. For Par Consols only 1841 figures are available.*[232]

Mine	Year	Number of Women
Fowey Consols	1836	308
Charlestown Mines	1836	120
Par Consols	1841	160
East Crinnis Mine	1836	46

Women were involved in all the procedures used to dress the ore when it reached the surface, except for the initial breaking up of the large pieces of mineral-bearing ore. This was done by men using a 14lb sledgehammer, called a ragging hammer. Once ragging was completed, women and girls took over the work. First came spalling, when the rock was broken down into smaller, fist-sized pieces by

---

230 'Consols' is the abbreviation for Consolidated Mines, so named when a number of mines amalgamated – or consolidated – under a single ownership.
231 Mayers, Lynne. *The St Austell Bal Maidens: Women and Girls at the Mines and Clay Works.* Cinderford: Blaize Bailey Books, 2011, pp.2–4.
232 Ibid., p.3.

Bal Maidens Spalling Ore, from Henderson, James. On the Methods Generally Adopted in Cornwall in Dressing Tin and Copper Ore, *presented to the Institution of Civil Engineers in 1858.*

women using a 5–7lb long-handled spalling hammer.

Then came cobbing, when the spalled rocks were broken into nut-sized pieces by teenage girls. Then the youngest girls worked at the picking tables, where they picked out the cobbed rocks with the greatest metal content. The waste pieces of rock – those with no metal content – were thrown into boxes on the floor, while the mixed-grade pieces were left on the table to be swept up by the older girls and taken to an anvil where women pounded the pieces into powder with small hammers – a process known as bucking. The resulting powder was then taken for separation, some to the buddles – shallow inclined troughs through which water flowed and separated the copper from the waste, and some to the jigging boxes – large mechanically or hand-operated sieves set in a tank of water.

It was hard physical work, which often damaged a bal maiden's health. Hammering and carrying heavy loads of ore or waste material caused muscular aches and pains. Feet and legs continually exposed to water when washing the ore developed rheumatism. The breaking down of the rocks filled the air with dust, and lung diseases were common. The continuous noise made by the bucking and cobbing processes led to deafness and also made it hard to hear conversation, although some bal maidens invented their own sign language so that they could communicate while they worked.

In spite of the challenges and health hazards, many bal maidens developed the strength, stamina, and technical ability needed to succeed as surface workers, and they showed a pride in their work which is reflected in the words of their chant:

> I can buddy and I can rocky
> And I can walk like a man
> I can looby and shaky
> And please the old Jan.[233]

Buddy means to work the buddles. Rocky, to break rocks. Looby, to toss ore. Shaky probably refers to operating the jigging boxes. The old Jan was the manager in charge of the surface workers, who was also known as the grass captain.

Women who were able to do surface work successfully and to 'walk like a man,' managed to assert their independence and establish a level of equality with male mine workers. Unsurprisingly this confident attitude received sharp criticism from those who believed that women should be confined to the domestic sphere.[234] One such

---

[233] Payton, Philip. 'Bal Maidens and Cousin Jenny: The Paradox of Women in Australia's Historic Mining Communities.' In *Australia, Migration and Empire: Immigrants in a Globalised World*, eds. Philip Payton and Andrekos Varnava, p.210. Camden: Palgrave Macmillan, 2019.

[234] Ibid., p.210.

was George Henwood, who visited mines in Cornwall between 1857 and 1859 and wrote of his severe disapproval of the bal maidens' lifestyle:

> *The indiscriminate association, in their employment, of the sexes naturally begets a want of modesty and delicacy, so important in the formation of character; whilst the masculine labour which females are frequently compelled to undertake, together with their being so long from home, render them wholly unfit to perform and attend to those domestic duties which should constitute the comfort and charm of every home.*[235]

Five of these skilled, independent, and physically strong women arrived in 1840 on Virgin Gorda, where they would work, just as in Cornwall, to dress the ore brought to the surface of the mine. One of them was Louisa Bovey, born near the market town of Totnes in Devon[236] in about 1818. She was the wife of William Tillar, a copper miner born in the village of Kea, about 17 miles (27km) from St Austell, who had settled in Tywardreath – a village about 5miles (8km) from St Austell. After their marriage, Louisa joined William in his cottage in Tywardreath, and there gave birth to a daughter, Elizabeth, in about 1836. When they left for Virgin Gorda Elizabeth, then four years old, went with them.

When they landed on the small island, the Tillars and the other

---

235 Henwood, George. *Cornwall's Mines and Miners: Nineteenth Century Studies.* Truro: Bradford Barton, 1972, p.118. (First published in the *Mining Journal* between June 1857 and May 1859 under the title 'Cornish Mine Photographs and Cornish Mining Maxims'.)

236 Louisa Bovey was not 'born Cornish', but as she married a Cornishman and spent most of her life in Cornwall, where all but one of her children were born, I have included her in this chapter.

Cornish miners and their families moved into cottages which had been built for them on a hill to the north of the mining operations. Mining companies in Cornwall did not usually provide housing for their employees, so the women likely saw the provision of accommodation in newly built cottages as a major improvement over their living conditions in Cornwall, where many lived in housing that was often damp and rundown. If the women settled easily into their cottages, there are other aspects of life on Virgin Gorda that they would have found more of a challenge, among these the need to acclimatise to the heat and the mosquitoes, and to familiarise themselves with the foods available in the local markets – which they then had to learn to prepare and cook using unfamiliar recipes and cooking techniques.

In addition to employing the Cornish miners and their wives, the mining company provided jobs for some of the local population, many of whom had only recently become free, and as the Cornish bal maidens dressed the ore they worked alongside the local women, helping them to learn the skills they needed. For white women to do physical labour alongside black women was not generally acceptable to Victorian society – George Henwood would surely not have approved – and is reminiscent of the days of indentured servitude, when Cornish women had gone out to the Caribbean to do physical labour and often worked with black enslaved women, the difference now being that the local workers were not enslaved, as their predecessors had been.

When the Cornish women worked, they probably wore the clothes they had been accustomed to wear at the St Austell mines. A large bonnet, a gook, protected them from rain, from flying shards of ore and – most importantly now they were on Virgin Gorda – from the tropical sun. An old dress, or a calf-length skirt of strong material, along with sturdy boots or shoes, ensured that they could work relatively safely among the ore and waste rocks that surrounded them. Hands were protected by homemade gloves and arms by long sleeves, and if they were doing the bucking they protected their legs with waterproofed leg protectors known as kitty bags, or leg coverings made of woven ropes of straw known as thumblebinds, or thumblebeans.[237]

Perhaps because their work clothes had to be so very practical and hard-wearing, the bal maidens were renowned for dressing well when they took part in the social events that provided a welcome diversion from mine work. Sunday worship provided another opportunity for mining women to wear their best clothes and on Virgin Gorda, where Wesleyan Methodism was well established, the bal maidens and their families, who were most likely Methodists, would have gone to the Methodist chapel in Spanish Town, the main centre of population on the island. Here the form of service was not much different from a Cornish service and here, dressed in their best clothes, they could feel at home and part of the community.

In its first year the mine produced ore that was assayed as containing a high percentage of copper – between 25 per cent and 50 per cent from June 1840 to June 1841 – and the President of the Virgin Islands was confident that the mine would live up to its early promise, providing a welcome boost to the local economy. Reporting to the Governor of the Leeward Islands, who was based in Antigua, he writes that a:

new channel of industry for the inhabitants and a fresh source of benefit to the colony has been opened in this enterprise which

---

237 Ibid., p.49.

may be regarded as giving fair promise for the future prospects of these islands.[238]

The closure of the mine towards the end of March 1842 was therefore – to the president at least – quite unexpected, but although the prospects had been good, the investors had unfortunately over-extended themselves to develop the mine infrastructure and they had run out of money. On its closure, the accounts showed that the ore produced had so far covered only one third of the cost of running the mine.[239]

At that point, all the Cornish miners and their families, including Louisa and her husband William and daughter Elizabeth, left the island. Louisa gave birth to a son, Charles, in about 1844, but there is some uncertainty as to whether he was born on Virgin Gorda or on the nearby island of St Thomas; the 1861 England and Wales census lists him as born on Virgin Gorda,[240] but the 1851 England and Wales census lists him as born on St Thomas.[241] The latter is a more likely place of birth, as by 1844 the mine had been closed and the family would have left Virgin Gorda to take a ship back to England, most likely via St Thomas. Remarkably, given the high mortality rate from tropical diseases in many parts of the Caribbean, all the miners and their families survived to return home, with the mine agent reporting

---

238 Burt, R. 'Virgin Gorda Copper Mine 1839–1862'. *Industrial Archaeology Review*, p.58 (Vol.6 Issue 1, 1981).

239 Birchall, Frank and Margaret Birchall. 'The Virgin Gorda Copper Mine, British Virgin Islands', p.25. *Journal of the Trevithick Society* (No.20, 1993).

240 The National Archives of the UK. Public Record Office. *Census Returns of England and Wales, 1861, Charles Tillar*; Class: RG 9; Piece: 1527; Folio: 27; Page 21; GSU roll: 542826.

241 The National Archives of the UK. Public Record Office. *Census Returns of England and Wales, 1851, Charles Tillar*; Class: H0107; Piece: 1905; Folio: 28; Page: 16: GSU roll: 221057.

that he 'had only one death in three years and that was an infant of about six weeks of age, sickly from birth'.[242]

The Tillar family settled back into life in Cornwall, and Louisa gave birth to a further six children – four girls and two boys – while William continued to make a living as a miner. Louisa eventually moved north to Usworth, near the city of Durham, where her husband, although now in his seventies, had gone to find employment in the coal mines. Perhaps during the cold, dark Usworth winters she thought back to the more pleasant climate of Virgin Gorda.

During the following years there were several attempts to reopen the Virgin Gorda copper mine, but all failed to operate at a profit and the mine closed for the last time in 1862, when the most recent group of Cornish miners employed at the mine – none of whom had brought their wives and children with them – returned to Cornwall, or moved on to other employment opportunities available in the mining world.

About 40 miles (64km) to the east of Virgin Gorda lies the small island of Sombrero. Only 0.9 miles (1.4km) long and 0.25 miles (0.4km) wide it had been named Sombrero by the Spanish because its shape reminded them of a hat. In 1825 a British Geological Survey team found large deposits of guano[243] on the islet but made no attempt to exploit it until, under the 1856 United States Guano Act, Sombrero was claimed by the United States and a US company began mining operations on the island. After some lengthy diplomatic negotiations Britain regained possession of Sombrero and awarded mining rights to the Sombrero Company, which shipped out over 100,000 tons of guano before running into financial difficulties and

---

242 *Letter of P.J. Minvielle to Julius Price, 22 April 1847, St Thomas, Virgin Islands.* Baring Archive. HC5 5.13.1 1847.
243 Accumulated layers of seabird excrement, valuable as an effective fertiliser.

liquidating the company in 1875. A new company, the New Sombrero Phosphate Company, was then established.

The superintendent employed by the New Sombrero Phosphate Company to run the mine was a Cornish mine captain, Thomas Corfield, who arrived on Sombrero accompanied by his wife, Mary Emma Pearce, born in Liskeard in 1847, and his eldest daughter Emmaline, born in Llanidloes, Wales, in 1870. The family settled into the Superintendent's House, a wooden bungalow surrounded by a wide veranda situated near the middle of the island, but Mary Emma spent little time there. As the miners broke up the phosphate the house reverberated to the continual din of the blasting, while the foul-smelling guano dust blew across the island and settled on everything in its path. Unsurprisingly, Mary Emma found managing the Superintendent's House in such an environment not to her liking, and lived mainly on the nearby islands of St Maarten and St Christopher. It was on these islands that she gave birth to five children: Bertha Elizabeth was born in 1876 on St Maarten, but sadly died in the same year; Thomas Joseph was born on St Maarten a year later; Richard Cecil was born on St Christopher in 1879; Dora was born on St Maarten in 1883; and Bessie on St Christopher in 1885.

St Maarten and St Christopher not only provided Mary Emma with a pleasanter environment in which to bring her children into the world, but they offered her a social life that was almost completely lacking on Sombrero, so she chose to lead a relatively independent life from her Sombrero-based husband. He died at the early age of forty-one on St Maarten, and was buried there, leaving his wife and children to return to Llanidloes. Mary Emma later moved from Llanidloes to Wigan in Lancashire, where she died in 1903.[244] Neither

---

244 Appleby, Sue. *The Cornish in the Caribbean: From the 17th to the 19th Centuries.*

Dora, Mary Emma's St Maarten-born daughter, nor Bessie, born in St Kitts, married, and both returned to Cornwall. Bessie became an elementary school teacher and Dora later returned to live in St Day, her father's place of birth, where she died in 1956.

If the Virgin Gorda mine was remarkable for the low rate of mortality among the miners and their families, the mines of Cuba were known for the opposite reason. Here the mortality rate was high, and at the El Cobre mines, which lay in the mountains of the Sierra del Cobre in the island's eastern region of Oriente, about 10 miles (16km) from the regional capital of Santiago de Cuba, deaths from yellow fever and other tropical diseases were common. Many Cornish miners who went to work there did not survive long.

The mining history of El Cobre goes back to the early days of Spain's colonisation of Cuba, when the Spanish Crown awarded the

Santiago de Cuba in 1856.

Kibworth Beauchamp: Matador, 2019, pp.252–255.

mining rights to a private contractor who mined the copper using African enslaved labour. When the contractor failed to develop the mine and little copper was produced, the Crown took over El Cobre and the enslaved workers became the property of the Spanish king: the King's Slaves. The colonial administration took little interest in the mine and the community, largely left to their own devices, began to develop their own small surface mining enterprises. Independent entrepreneurial activity by enslaved people on a community level was certainly unusual, but what made El Cobre unique was that the miners were mostly women. Throughout the late 17th and most of the 18th century these women succeeded in producing enough copper to supply the domestic market, and continued to do so after they were freed by a Royal Decree in 1801 – a decree that guaranteed them against a return to enslavement and established the community's right to exploit the local copper resources. The El Cobre women continued to supply the island's copper requirements until the rapid development of the sugar industry – with its need for a steady supply of the large round coppers used to boil the sugar cane juice – made it necessary to import copper from Mexico.

In the 1830s, after Britain had lifted tariffs on imported ore, mainly British investors took over and developed the mines, and the industry moved from being a small local enterprise to a large export-oriented foreign-owned business using sophisticated mining technology.[245] The two main British-owned companies who mined at El Cobre were La Compañía Consolidada de Minas del Cobre (The Cobre Mines Consolidated Company) – known locally as La Compañía Consolidada, and El Real de Santiago (The Royal Santiago Mining

---

245 Díaz, María Elena, 'Mining Women, Royal Slaves: Copper Mining in Colonial Cuba, 1670–1780.' In *Mining Women: Gender in the Development of a Global industry, 1670 to 2005*, eds. Jaclyn J. Gier-Viskovatoff and Laurie Mercier, pp.21–23. New York: Palgrave Macmillan, 2006.

Company). Both companies brought in miners from Cornwall, many from the Redruth area, and initially mine managers preferred to employ young single men with no family responsibilities to distract them from their work. But in 1843 a number of miners were arrested after going on strike for better wages, and after their release caused disruption by getting violently drunk and fighting. After this event the mine management began to rethink its policy, reasoning – like the Methodist Missionary Society – that men who left home with a wife were more likely to lead a steady life and be reliable workers than bachelors with a tendency to wild behaviour. Married men were now encouraged to come to El Cobre.

Despite the health risks, some Cornish women did accompany their husbands to Cuba. One was Jenifer Williams. Always known as Jane rather than Jenifer, she had been born in the mining town of Redruth in about 1813, and married Zacharias Johns, also from Redruth, in 1834. Their first child, Mary Ann, was born in Redruth a year later. Zacharias was a copper miner and, perhaps out of work or attracted by the wages offered by the El Cobre mine owners, he left his wife and daughter for Cuba shortly after Mary Ann was born. Jane joined him some time later, taking Mary Ann with her, and in 1845 she gave birth to a second daughter, Elizabeth Jane, at El Cobre.[246]

She would have lived in one of the single-storey houses built for the miners close to the mine, and on the edge of what had grown from a small settlement to a sizeable community of miners. The house Jane managed was of a typically Spanish colonial design, very different from the stone Cornish cottage she was accustomed to.

---

246 Information on Jane Williams and her family provided by Di Donovan in email dated 19 April 2021.

Constructed of adobe,[247] with wooden roof beams and overlapping ceramic roof tiles, her house, like the others, was painted in bright colours. Windows were protected with adjustable wooden louvres on the inside and iron bars on the outside. The louvres could be closed at night, when rain fell, or when a hurricane threatened, but the windows had no glass, so when the louvres were left open for ventilation in the hot and humid tropical climate, not only breezes but mosquitoes blew into the house, including those carrying the dreaded yellow fever.

If Jane found the ever-present threat of sickness and death from infectious tropical diseases hard to come to terms with, experiencing the reality of enslaved labour for the first time must have been even more of a challenge. The enslaved in the British Caribbean had been emancipated in 1834, and under the terms of the Anglo-Spanish Treaty of 1817 it was illegal to ship enslaved people to Cuba, but in countries that were not under British jurisdiction – such as Cuba – it was still legal to own enslaved people. The Cuban plantocracy in any case often ignored the treaty because there was a high demand for enslaved labour to work the growing sugar and coffee industries, and shipments of enslaved Africans continued to arrive on Cuba's shores. With such a large labour force available, planters were willing to rent their human property out to the mining companies as and when they were needed. The treatment they received must have shocked Jane just as it did the miner James Whitburn who, soon after arriving at El Cobre, wrote in his diary:

> *The flogging of the negroes in this country is most cruel. I have seen them laid on the ground, sometimes tied to a ladder, and at other times held by one man at the foot and another at the head,*

---

247 Adobe is made of mud bricks dried in the sun.

while another negro with a whip 10 or 12ft. long from the end of the stick to the point of the lash, gives the negro confined 25 blows or I may say, cuts with the aforementioned whip, and, while every blow rattles almost as loud as a gun, I have seen I think from 15 blows out of 25 to make cuts in the flesh from 8 to 12 inches long and open as if done with a knife.[248]

Less shocking but equally strange to the Cornish women and their families, most of whom were Wesleyan Methodists, were the religious observances of the El Cobre community. Roman Catholicism was the official religion of Cuba, as it was for the rest of the Spanish Empire, and El Cobre, as well as being an important mine, was renowned as the Roman Catholic sanctuary of Nuestra Señora Caridad del Cobre (Our Lady of Charity of Cobre), the patron saint of Cuba. When the people of El Cobre worshipped their patron saint, colonial Roman Catholic practices were intertwined with the Afro-Cuban beliefs of the enslaved and free people of colour in the community, and to many Cubans Our Lady of Charity was – and indeed still is – both Our Lady, Mother of Jesus, and Ochún, or Oshún, the Yoruban Mother Goddess.[249] James Whitburn records his reaction after experiencing a church service at El Cobre in mid-December:

About a fortnight before Christmas a great number of people attend the church... The priest commences with reading something in Latin... [and] I was surprised to hear several rattles break out all at once, with a tremendous noise, while others were blowing

---
248 Whitburn, James. *A Cornish Man in Cuba: Transcript of a Diary of his Visit to Cuba 1836–1838*. np: Whitburn, nd, p.4.
249 Díaz, María Elena. *The Virgin, the King, and the Royal Slaves of El Cobre: Negotiating Freedom in Colonial Cuba, 1670–1780*. Stanford: Stanford University Press, 2000, p.1.

into something which made a noise similar to that of a bullock horn [perhaps a conch shell] in England and others shrieking and yelling while the Priest was sanctifying the wine… how different from thee oh happy England.[250]

After several years in Cuba, Jane and her husband and family returned to Cornwall, and by 1850 they were again living in Redruth. They were not alone in leaving the island at this time, as during the 1840s, '50s, and '60s several events and developments impacted the ability of the El Cobre mining companies to operate at a profit and then, as conditions at the mine deteriorated, they began to lay off employees.

One of those events was the passage of several severe hurricanes which hit the island during the June to October hurricane seasons of 1842, 1844, and 1846. Terrifying to live through, they also damaged the mining infrastructure and disrupted the mining operations and the shipment of ore. Mining was further disrupted by increased Cuban demands for independence from Spain, leading to several uprisings during the 1840s which were supported by broad cross-sections of the population including free people of colour, local intellectuals, planters, and businesspeople, and were put down with great severity by the colonial administration. At the same time – and most importantly for the mining companies – the copper content of the ore which had made the El Cobre mines such a lucrative investment began to fall until it was no longer economical to ship the ore from the port at Santiago to Swansea in Wales to be smelted. The first mine to fail was El Real de Santiago; it began operating at a loss in 1848 and, following the collapse of the mine's engine shaft, which

---

250 Whitburn, James. *A Cornish Man in Cuba: Transcript of a Diary of his Visit to Cuba 1836–1838*. np: Whitburn, nd, p.3.

the company did not have the finances to rebuild, the mine closed in 1858.

In spite of the Spanish government's efforts to crush the Cuban independence movement, it continued to strengthen and in 1865 its supporters began to make specific demands for tariff reform, Cuban representation in Parliament, judicial equality with Spaniards, and full enforcement of the official ban on the trade in enslaved people, which came into effect in 1867. Spain responded by attempting to ban all attempts at liberal reform and by increasing the taxation of local planters and businesspeople. This caused more widespread unrest, especially among the powerful local plantation and estate owners in eastern Cuba, and saw the beginning of the Ten Years' War for Cuban independence from Spain, led by Carlos Manuel de Céspedes, a wealthy plantation owner from Bayamo, a city no more than 60 miles (97km) from El Cobre. As the fighting began, the families living at El Cobre found themselves in the middle of confrontations between Spanish and *Independentista* forces, and with their lives frequently in danger of being cut short as they tried to go about their daily lives many decided to leave.

La Compañía Consolidada managed to continue after the closure of El Real de Santiago, but as the copper content of the ore mined there continued to fall, the river that was the essential source of water to run the steam engines and for dressing the ore dried up, and fighting continued in the area, it became almost impossible for the company to operate. The monthly payroll then became target for the *Independentistas*, and when the money arrived at the port of Santiago it was a challenge for the mining company to move it from the port to the accounting office so the workforce could be paid. Conditions deteriorated further when the five bridges that carried the railway – the only means of transport between the port and El Cobre – were destroyed in the fighting. As the Ten Years' War brought increasing dislocation to its mining operations, La Compañía Consolidada had no option but to close, and it ceased operations in 1869.[251]

Back home in Redruth, Jane Williams' husband, Zacharias Johns, changed occupation from miner to farmer. He worked ten acres of land and became a beer seller, while Jane gave birth to two more children; a daughter, Catherine, born in 1850, and a son, Zacharias, born in 1853. A few years later Zacharias Senior, regretting his decision to return to Redruth, went back to Cuba, leaving Jane to adjust to life as a 'married widow' – a married woman whose miner husband went to earn a living wherever in the world there was a work opportunity, leaving her to make a life for herself for however long her spouse was absent. Sometimes a husband never returned to his wife, and Zacharias may have been one of their number, as it is uncertain whether he ever went back to Jane before he migrated to Bendigo, Victoria, South Australia, where he worked as a gold miner until his death in early 1875.

Jane remained in Redruth and supported herself as a dressmaker and needlewoman, but research has so far failed to provide information about her last years. Elizabeth Jane, the daughter Jane had given birth to at El Cobre, married William Hicks in Redruth in 1873, and the couple had two children, William and Elizabeth Jane, before moving to South Australia in late 1884. Elizabeth Jane gave birth to two additional children in Walleroo – Edith Rosaline in 1885 and Effie Evelyn in 1889 – and the family remained in Walleroo, where William died in 1924 and Elizabeth Jane in 1931.[252]

At about the same time as Jane went out to Cuba to join her

---

251 Schwartz, Sharron P. *The Cornish in Latin America: 'Cousin Jack' and the New World*. Wicklow: Cornubian Press, 2016, pp.114–115.

252 Information on Jane Williams and her family provided by Di Donovan in email dated 19 April 2021.

husband Zacharias, Susan Palmer, born in the village of Veryan in about 1821 and married to Richard May from nearby Tregony, accompanied her husband to El Cobre. Richard was a blacksmith, a trade always much in demand at the mines, where his skills would have been an important part of helping to ensure that the mine continued to function, and where he would have made and repaired the many metal objects that were vital to mine work. Susan had her first three babies at El Cobre – Solomon Palmer in 1849, Charles in 1852, and Susan Mary in 1853. Two years later the family were back in Cornwall, settling in the St Agnes mining area, and here Susan gave birth to Catherine in 1855 before moving to Tuckingmill, where John was born in 1858, followed by William in 1860 and Jane in 1863. By 1891 Susan and her husband Richard were living with their daughter Catherine and her husband – a blacksmith like Richard – in Crowan, a village near the mining town of Camborne, and here Susan died in 1905.[253]

In addition to the Cornish miners' wives who went to El Cobre were the Cornish women married to senior El Cobre employees. They lived a more comfortable existence than the women married to the regular miners, occupying substantial residences – rather than the small adobe houses occupied by the miners and their families – which they managed with the assistance of a number of servants. One of these senior wives was Elizabeth Opie, born in the village of Tywardreath in 1804. She was the wife of Daniel McKenny (sometimes spelt McKenney), one of El Cobre's resident mine agents. The couple married in 1824 and settled in Redruth, where Elizabeth gave birth to six children: Samuel in 1825, Daniel in 1827, Isaac in 1830, Jacob in 1832 (who died in his infancy), another son

---

253 Information on Susan Palmer and her family based on information provided by Lesley Trotter in email dated 30 March 2014.

named Jacob in 1834, and Elizabeth Marianne in 1837. In late 1842 Elizabeth set sail for Cuba to join her husband, and although we do not know how many of her children accompanied her to Cuba, most likely the younger ones would have done so. Once settled at El Cobre their education would have been their mother's responsibility and, like the Wesleyan missionary wives, she would have taught them as best she could, depending on the texts available and her own ability to teach. Elizabeth spent five years living at El Cobre, giving birth – at the age of forty – to a daughter, Mary, in 1845. The family left Cuba in 1847 and returned to Redruth where, in the same year, Elizabeth's daughter Caroline was born.

Daniel did not spend long in Redruth. Although described as 'of the Parish of Redruth in the County of Cornwall, Mine Agent' in the will he made on 27 December 1847,[254] he boarded the ship *Lady Prudhoe* when she left Swansea bound for Cuba in October 1848. Unfortunately, however, he died en route, reportedly of a 'severe cold'.[255] The following year Elizabeth suffered another loss, when her son Daniel, who sailed from Liverpool to start a new life in the United States, died en route to Philadelphia.

If she had remained a widow Elizabeth would have been well provided for by the terms of her husband's will which states:

> *My wife Elizabeth McKenny shall enjoy and manage my leasehold premises… for her maintenance and the maintenance and duration of my dear children and receive the interest on my money deposited in the aforesaid Cornish Bank Redruth. If my wife Elizabeth McKenny marry or live with any man my will*

---

254 Information on the McKenny family provided by Ross Garner in email dated 24 April 2021.
255 Ibid.

is that my children take charge of my property… My will is that in the event of my wife marrying or living with a man she shall not have anything to do with my property or my children but that my children Samuel, Daniel, Isaac, Jacob, Elizabeth, Mary and Caroline McKenny take charge of and manage my property.[256]

As a widow, Elizabeth was free from the restrictions of coverture, and had control over her financial affairs, but three years after Daniel's death she chose to marry Thomas John in Redruth, thus forfeiting the provisions made for her by her first husband. But Elizabeth's children may not have had the skills necessary to 'take charge and manage' their father's property, as when Elizabeth remarried, instead of taking responsibility for their inheritance, they began to leave home in search of new opportunities. Elizabeth's son Daniel left for the United States a year after his father's death, and in 1854 her son Jacob left to seek employment in Australia. Elizabeth moved to Penzance with her second husband, but he died in 1856, leaving her a widow for a second time.

The family's financial situation appears to have continued to deteriorate after the death of Elizabeth's second husband, as by 1861 fifteen-year-old Mary, Elizabeth's Cuban-born daughter, was working as a children's nursemaid and had few opportunities for advancement. With little to lose, the women of the family – Elizabeth, then fifty-six, along with daughters Mary and Caroline and stepdaughter Mary John – made the decision to join Elizabeth's son Jacob in Australia, perhaps using whatever was left of Daniel McKenny's inheritance to fund their passage. Their ship left Plymouth for Melbourne, landing in March 1862, but Elizabeth unfortunately died just twelve days

---

256 Ibid.

Mary McKenny, image courtesy of Ross Garner.

after their arrival, leaving Mary, aged sixteen, and Caroline and Mary John, both aged fourteen, to find their way in a new country.

By 1867 Mary McKenny was living in Ballarat, Victoria, where she met Andrew Melrose, a Scot born in Edinburgh, Scotland, in 1842. She had his first child, Elizabeth Mary, in 1867, followed by Anne in 1867, Calville Oblair Graham in 1871, Andrew Herbert in 1873, and Mary in 1875. After marrying Andrew at the Wesleyan Parsonage in Creswick, Victoria, in 1876, she continued to have more children: Daniel Curtis in 1877, Helen Caroline in 1879, James Alexander in 1881, Benjamin in 1883, and William Harold in 1885, when she was thirty-nine years old. Of her ten children, three – Mary, Benjamin, and Daniel – did not survive their early years.

She probably had few memories of her early life in Cuba but, like so many Cornish men and women who left Cornwall during the 19th century for opportunities elsewhere, she made a new life in Australia along with her brother Jacob, while brother Samuel and sister Elizabeth Marianne moved to New Zealand, and brother Isaac to the United States. Mary died in 1906, aged sixty-one.

Elizabeth Ann Manderson was another mine agent's wife who

went out to the El Cobre mines with her husband. She had been born in St Mawes, a coastal village near Falmouth, in 1809, and in 1829 she married James Treweek, a miner born in Gwennap in 1807. James was employed by the El Real de Santiago mine, and by the time the family travelled out to Cuba Elizabeth Ann had given birth to four sons: John Henry Martin in 1830, James Manderson in 1831, Nicholas in 1834, and Francis in 1837. Two daughters were born at El Cobre: Jane Abigail in 1842 and Elizabeth Ann in 1844.

The family returned to Cornwall in 1847 and settled in Gwennap, where a son, William Tiddy, was born. He was christened on 6 June 1847, and – unusually at a time when infant mortality was high, so babies were christened as early as possible after their birth – his five-year-old sister Jane Abigail and three-year-old sister Elizabeth Ann were christened along with him. The reason the two girls born in Cuba had not been christened as infants, was because the Treweeks were Protestants and did not want their children baptised into the Roman Catholic faith. Roman Catholicism was then the official and only recognised religion in Cuba – as it was in Spain and all its colonies – and the only way Protestants could be legally christened, married, and buried in Cuba was if they professed to be Catholic.[257] Elizabeth McKenny's brother-in-law William, who died at El Cobre, was one Protestant who, according to his death record, converted to Roman Catholicism just before his death so that he could receive a Christian burial. His death record, translated from the Spanish, reads in part:

---

257 Martínez-Fernández, Luis. '"Don't Die Here": the Death and Burial of Protestants in the Hispanic Caribbean, 1840–1885.' *The Americas*, pp.23–47 (Vol.49, No.1, July 1992).

> [In the] year of the Lord 1837, ninth of October, Francisco Ramon Ramón de Vega Mustelier, priest in charge at the Holy Parish Church of Santiago del Prado Real at the Mines of El Cobre, gave Christian burial… to the adult Mr Guillermo Maquini [note the Spanish spelling of his name] about nineteen years old… who died in communion with the Holy Mother Church and [after] reception of the Holy Sacraments of Penance and Extreme Unction.[258]

Given the high death rate at El Cobre, and the expense of shipping the dead back home, the mining companies – with financial rather than humanitarian concerns foremost in their minds – managed to negotiate with the colonial administration for permission to open a Protestant burial ground near the mine and from then on, although the arrangements were basic and the ground overcrowded, it provided a place of burial for those miners and their families who chose not to convert to Roman Catholicism.

Back in Cornwall, after giving birth to William, Elizabeth Ann gave birth to a daughter, Ann Curgenven, born in 1848, but who died in the same year, and an additional son, George Manderson, born in 1849. When her husband retired from the mining industry, he became a landowner in Mawnan, farming 60 acres, and moving into the residence known as Chatham Cottage with his family. Elizabeth Ann's elder Cuban-born daughter, Jane Abigail, married Colonel Francis Henry Pender of the King's Own Borderers at the late age of thirty-eight. Having grown up as the daughter of a mine agent – one of the Middling Sort – after her marriage she moved to Budock Vean, the seat of the Pender family, and settled into her new life as a Lady of Quality. Elizabeth Ann's younger Cuban-born daughter,

---

258 Translated death record provided by Ross Garner.

Elizabeth Ann, married Thomas West, a Cornish-born customs officer whose first wife had died ten years previously. Neither Jane Abigail nor Elizabeth Ann had any children.[259]

Of the Cornish miners' wives included in this chapter, Amelia Pascoe was the most widely travelled. She had been born in Truro in 1813 and, in early 1834 married John Holman, born in Kenwyn in 1808. Soon after their marriage Amelia accompanied her husband, who earned his living as a tin miner at the time of their marriage, to one of the mines in South America. Here their first child, Eliza, was born in 1835, but she did not survive her infancy. The couple were back in Cornwall by 1838, when Amelia gave birth to a son, James, who died aged five, and a daughter, Ellen, born in 1841. By 1844 the family were in Jamaica where, given the year of their arrival, their destination was probably either the copper mine in the Port Royal Mountains in the Parish of St Andrews, which operated between 1840 and 1846,[260] or the one on Mount Vernon in the Parish of St Thomas, which functioned between 1841 and 1857.[261] Amelia gave birth to daughter Julia in Jamaica in 1844, and then by 1846 the family were on the move again, this time to Cuba, where John joined senior members of the El Cobre mining community as a mine agent.

Moving her three young children from the English-speaking Protestant society of Jamaica to the Spanish-speaking Roman Catholic society of Cuba must have been a challenge for Amelia, but fortunately, wives who accompanied their husbands to distant mines usually had the support of mining wives who had arrived before them to help them transition to a new culture. At the age of thirty-eight

---

259 Information on Elizabeth Ann Manderson and her family from data provided by Martin Wolfgang in correspondence dated 15 February 2023.

260 Appleby, Sue. *The Cornish in the Caribbean: From the 17th to the 19th Centuries.* Kibworth Beauchamp: Matador, 2019, p.61.

261 Ibid., pp.63–64.

Amelia gave birth to a daughter at El Cobre, who, like many but not all children born at mines in Spanish-speaking countries, was given a Spanish first name – Annetta. In 1849 a son was born, also at El Cobre, but unlike his sister he was given the English name of Charles.

The following year the family returned to Cornwall, and John Holman, like Zacharias John, decided on a change of career. He took up farming, working land in the hamlet of Parkhoskin (sometimes spelt Park Hosken or Hoskyn) near the village of Perranzabuloe, about 2 miles (3.2km) from the town of Perranporth on Cornwall's north coast. Amelia, now a farmer's wife, gave birth to two more sons, Edwin in 1850 and John James in 1853. In 1860 the family were saddened by the death of both nineteen-year-old Ellen and sixteen-year-old, Jamaica-born, Julia. Both died in the same year, and were perhaps the victims of some infectious disease. Infant and child mortality was still high in the 19th century and Amelia had now lost four of her children – Eliza as an infant in South America, James in Cornwall, aged five, and now Ellen and Julia. By 1871 John had the means to build Penwartha House and extend his land holdings. He now farmed 100 acres, assisted by his son John, while Cuban-born Charles farmed the neighbouring property. When her husband died at Penwartha House in 1875 Amelia moved back to Truro, living in a house in Pydar Street until her death in 1893. Amelia's only surviving daughter, Cuban-born Annetta, married Nicholas Bryant in 1870 and gave birth to a son, Sydney Seymour, the following year. Following the death of her first husband she married Luke Wilce in 1883 with whom she had a son, Leonard, the following year.[262]

Not all the Cornish living at El Cobre left Cuba when the mines closed. Jane Kemp, who had been born in Redruth in about 1825,

---

[262] Information on Amelia Pascoe and her family from data provided by Graham Lambert in correspondence dated 13 February 2023.

had married John Harvey, also from Redruth, and moved to Lanner, a village just to the south-east of Redruth, where she had given birth to seven children: Jane, born in 1842, Julianna, born in 1847 – who died aged six in 1853 – Theodore, born in 1848, Josiah, born in 1849, Frederick, born in 1851, William, born in 1853, and Albert, born in 1854. In 1855 the whole family had moved to El Cobre, where John was employed as a mining engineer and mine agent. In 1861 Jane gave birth to Carlos de la Caridad – note the Spanish first name given to the Cuba-born son – and all the Harvey children born in Lanner were re-baptised into the Roman Catholic faith, because John and Jane had decided to stay in Cuba and realised that there was little chance for their children to advance in life on the island unless they were Roman Catholics.[263] Jane unfortunately died of cholera in 1869, and following her death John Harvey married Dolores Guerra y Toledo.

Jane and John's firstborn daughter, Jane Harvey, married Edward Hodge, a mining engineer, at El Cobre, and the couple had two children there: Maria, born in 1867 and Edwin, born in 1868. Contrary to John's wish to have his family settle in Cuba, Jane and her husband Edward left the island soon after the birth of their son, and returned to Cornwall. By 1870 Jane was residing in the village of St Erth, along with her husband and other family members – including her young brothers Albert and Carlos, who had also left El Cobre – and in that year she gave birth to a daughter, Ellen Jane.[264] In the 1871 census her address is given as Foundry, and as her husband was an

---

[263] Information on the Harvey family from: Perez del Castillo, Guillermo. 'The Harvey Family in El Cobre.' *Revista: Cuban Genealogical Society*, pp.2–4 (Vol.15, January 2006).

[264] The National Archives of the UK. Public Record Office. *Census Returns of England and Wales, 1871.* Jane Hodge. Class: RG10; Piece: 2331; Folio: 36; Page: 16; GSU roll: 838828.

engineer he probably worked at Hayle Foundry, the biggest foundry in Cornwall during the 19th century.[265] What language did she speak at home? Most likely, especially when speaking with Carlos, it would have been a mixture of English and Spanish, a way of speaking that was common in many of the towns and villages of Cornwall where so many miners and their families had spent time working in Spanish-speaking countries.

Jane Kemp, like other 19th-century Cornish mining wives, had gone overseas to accompany her husband when he took up a work offer overseas. These women did not travel the world independently, and, when they arrived at a new destination, usually had little sense of purpose other than to provide their husband with a comfortable home and give birth to more children. One small group of mining women, the wives of the Virgin Gorda Cornish miners, were an exception. Over the years they spent working in Cornish mines these women, like many before them, had acquired the surface work skills, independent spirit, and sense of self-value that enabled them, as bal maidens, to make their way in a patriarchal society and a male-dominated mining industry. As they worked at the Virgin Gorda copper mine, they had a unique opportunity to pass on these skills and attributes to the women who worked alongside them – the recently enslaved local women looking to begin a new life as free people.

---

265 Ibid.

Bibliography

'An Eligible Situation at Marazion in Mount's-Bay.' *Royal Cornwall Gazette*, p.3 (26 May 1804).

Antigua and the Antiguans: A Full Account of the Colony and its Inhabitants from the Time of the Caribs to the Present Day Interspersed with Anecdotes and Legends. 2 vols. St John's: Antiguan Publishing Trust, 1980. Work attributed to a Mrs. Flannigan or Lanaghan, first published in 1844.

Appleby, Sue. *The Cornish in the Caribbean: From the 17th to the 19th Centuries*. Kibworth Beauchamp: Matador, 2019.

Beckles, Hilary MacDonald. *Centering Women: Gender Discourses in Caribbean Slave Society*. Kingston: Ian Randle, 1999.

Beckles, Hilary MacDonald. *Natural Rebels: A Social History of Enslaved Black Women in Barbados*. New Brunswick: Rutgers University Press, 1990.

Beckles, Hilary MacDonald. 'White Labour in Black Slave Plantation Society and Economy: A Case Study of Indentured Labour in Seventeenth Century Barbados.' PhD diss., University of Hull, 1980.

Beckles, Hilary MacDonald. *White Servitude and Black Slavery in Barbados, 1627–1715*. Knoxville: University of Tennessee Press, 1989.

Beckles, Hilary MacDonald. 'White Women and Slavery in the Caribbean.' *History Workshop Journal*, pp.66–82 (Vol. 36, Issue 1, Autumn 1993). Accessed 24 August 2021, https://doi.org/10.1093/hwj/36.1.66

Bennett, Christian C. 'Women's Work: The Role of Women in Wesleyan Methodist Overseas Mission in the Nineteenth Century.' *Methodist History*, pp.229–236 (Vol.32, No.4, July 1994).

Bennett, Dennis Stanley Lanyon. *William Lanyon Bennett, Born 1856: His Life Story*. Unpublished notes, 1982.

Birchall, Frank and Margaret Birchall. 'The Virgin Gorda Copper Mine, British Virgin Islands.' *Journal of the Trevithick Society* (No.20, 1993).

Blake, Colin and Feock Parish Council. *Feock Trails – History Information: Historic Houses – Trelissick*. Accessed 15 November 2021, https://www.feockpc.com/trelissick

Blewett Family: Henry Blewett 1836–1891. Accessed 10 October 2022, http://www.mygenealogies.co.uk/Blewett/BLEW-B3.htm

Brathwaite, Kamau. *The Development of Creole Society in Jamaica, 1770–1820*. Kingston, Ian Randle, 2005.

Brereton, Bridget. 'Gendered Testimonies: Autobiographies, Diaries and Letters by Women as Sources for Caribbean History.' *Feminist Review*, pp.143–163 (Vol.59, No.1, June 1998).

Brereton, Bridget. 'Women and Gender in Caribbean (English-Speaking) Historiography.' *Clio: Women, Gender, History*, pp.211–240 (Vol.50, No.2, June 2019).

Brunache, Peggy. *Slave Rebellion in the Eighteenth Century: Tacky's Revolt*. Glasgow: University of Glasgow, [2020]. Accessed 15 October 2021, https://www.futurelearn.com/info/courses/slavery-in-the-british-caribbean/0/steps/162134

Bryan, Patrick E. *The Jamaican People, 1880–1902: Race, Class, and Social Control*. London: Macmillan Caribbean, 1991.

Buckley, Allen. *Cornish Bal Maidens*. Redruth: Tor Mark, 2010.

Bundy, David. 'The African and Caribbean Origins of Methodism in the Bahamas.' *Methodist History*, pp.173–183 (Vol.53, No.3, April 2015).

Burnard, Trevor. 'Inheritance and Independence: Women's Status in Early Colonial Jamaica.' *William and Mary Quarterly*, pp.93–111 (Vol.48, No.1, January 1991).

Burnard, Trevor. *Mastery, Tyranny, and Desire: Thomas Thistlewood and His Slaves in the Anglo-Jamaican World*. Chapel Hill: University of North Carolina Press, 2004.

Burt, R. 'Virgin Gorda Copper Mine 1839–1862'. *Industrial Archaeology Review*. (Vol.6 Issue 1, 1981).

Bush, Barbara. *Slave Women in Caribbean Society, 1650–1838*. Kingston: Heinemann Publishers (Caribbean), 1990.

Bush, Barbara. 'White "Ladies", Coloured "Favourites" and Black "Wenches": Some Considerations on Sex, Race and Class Factors in Social Relations in White Creole Society in the British Caribbean.' *Slavery & Abolition: A Journal of Slave and Post-Slave Studies*, pp.245–262 (Vol. 2, No.3, 1981).

Carey, Brycchan. 'From Guinea to Guernsey and Cornwall to the Caribbean: Recovering the History of Slavery in the Western English Channel.' In *Britain's Memory and Memory of Transatlantic Slavery: Local Nuances of a National Sin*, edited by Katie Donington, Ryan Hanley and Jessica Moody, pp.21–38. Liverpool: Liverpool University Press, 2016.

Carmichael, A.C. *Domestic Manners and Social Condition of the White, Coloured and Negro Population of the West Indies*. 2 vols. London: Whittaker Treacher and Co., 1833.

Coldham, Peter Wilson. *The Complete Book of Emigrants: 1607–1660*. Baltimore: Genealogical Publishing Company, 1987.

'Cornish Families: The Daniells.' In *One and All: A Cornish Monthly Illustrated Journal* (March 1869) p.11.

Cornwall Live. *From Slave Owners to Abolitionist Campaigners – Cornwall's Role in the Slave Trade*. Accessed 7 May 2021, https://www.cornwalllive.com/news/cornwall-news/slave-owners-abolitionist-campaigners-cornwalls-4236811

Courtney Library. *Cornish People Overseas from 1840: Index Compiled from Local Newspapers*. Truro: Courtney Library, nd.

Craton, Michael and James Walvin. *A Jamaican Plantation: The History of Worthy Park 1670–1970*. Toronto: University of Toronto Press, 1970.

Cundall, Frank. *Historic Jamaica; With Fifty-Two Illustrations*. London: West India Committee for the Institute of Jamaica, 1915. Accessed 14 November 2021, https://ia800207.us.archive.org/11/items/cu31924020417527/cu31924020417527.pdf

Cundall, Frank. 'The Press and Printers of Jamaica Prior to 1820.' *Proceedings* of the American Antiquarian Society, pp.290–354. (Vol.26, October 1916). Accessed 3 November 2021, https://www.americanantiquarian.org/proceedings/44806619.pdf

Deacon, Bernard. *Cornish Mining: A Short History.* Accessed 10 July 2023, https://bernarddeacon.com/mining/cornish-mining-a-short-history/

Devon Mitchells and Some Cornish too. Accessed November 2021, http://www.devon-mitchells.co.uk/showtree.php?tree=CornishMichells

Díaz, María Elena, 'Mining Women, Royal Slaves: Copper Mining in Colonial Cuba, 1670–1780.' In *Mining Women: Gender in the Development of a Global industry, 1670 to 2005,* edited by Jaclyn J. Gier-Viskovatoff and Laurie Mercier, pp.21–39. New York: Palgrave Macmillan, 2006.

Díaz, María Elena. *The Virgin, the King, and the Royal Slaves of El Cobre: Negotiating Freedom in Colonial Cuba, 1670–1780.* Stanford: Stanford University Press, 2000, p.1.

Dictionary of Methodism in Britain and Ireland: Women. Accessed 18 November 2022, https://dmbi.online/index.php?do=app.entry&id=3051

Dictionary of Methodism in Britain and Ireland: Women's Work. Accessed 16 December 2022, https://dmbi.online/index.php?do=app.entry&id=3054

Druett, Joan. *Hen Frigates: Wives of Merchant Captains Under Sail.* New York: Simon and Schuster, 1998.

du Quesnay, Frederick J. *The Longs of 'Longville'.* Accessed 12 October 2021, http://www.jamaicanfamilysearch.com/Samples/fred02.htm

Dyde, Brian. *Out of the Crowded Vagueness: A History of the Islands of St Kitts, Nevis and Anguilla.* Oxford: Macmillan Education, 2005.

Emmer, P.C. *Colonialism and Migration; Indentured Labour Before and After Slavery.* Dordrecht: Martinus Nijhoff, 1986.

English, John C. "Dear Sister:" John Wesley and the Women of Early Methodism.' *Methodist History,* pp.26–33 (Vol.33, No.1, October 1994).

Evans, Chris. 'Brazilian Gold, Cuban Copper and the Final Frontier of

British Anti-Slavery.' *Slavery and Abolition*, pp.118–134 (Vol.34, No.1, 2013).

Fawcett, William. 'The Public Gardens and Plantations of Jamaica.' *Botanical Gazette*, pp.345–69 (Vol.24, No. 5, 1897). Accessed 19 November 2021, http://www.jstor.org/stable/2464044.

Fenwick, Eliza. *Secresy or the Ruin on the Rock*. Peterborough: Broadview Press, 1994.

Fenwick, Eliza. *The Fate of the Fenwicks: Letters to Mary Hays (1798–1828)*. London: Methuen, 1927.

Fenwick, Eliza. *Visits to the Juvenile Library; or, Knowledge Proved to be the Source of Happiness*. London: Tabart and Co., 1805.

Findlay, G.G. and W.W. Holdsworth. *The History of the Wesleyan Methodist Missionary Society*. Vol.2. London: Epworth Press, 1921. Accessed 3 November 2011, https://ia800205.us.archive.org/17/items/historyofwesleya02finduoft/historyofwesleya02finduoft.pdf

Foster, Henry Blaine. *Rise and Progress of Wesleyan-Methodism in Jamaica*. London: Wesleyan Conference Office, 1881. Accessed 3 November 2022, https://books.google.com.ag/books?id=muoCAAAAQAAJ&printsec=frontcover&source=gbs_ge_summary_r&cad=0#v=onepage&q&f=false

Friends of the West Norwood Cemetery. *Lives of the Dead: A Self-Guided Walk Round West Norwood Cemetery*. London: Royal Geographical Society, 2014. Accessed 7 November 2022, https://www.discoveringbritain.org/content/discoveringbritain/walk%20booklets/West%20Norwood%20DB%20walk%20-%20written%20guide.pdf

Froude, James Anthony. *The English in the West Indies*. London: Longmans, Green and Company, 1888.

Galenson, David W. 'British Servants and the Colonial Indenture System in the Eighteenth Century.' *The Journal of Southern History*, pp.41–66 (Vol.44, No. 1,1978).

Galenson, David W. 'The Rise and Fall of Indentured Servitude in the Americas: An Economic Analysis.' *Journal of Economic History*, pp.1–26 (Vol.44, No.1, March 1984).

Gaspar, David Barry. *Bondsmen and Rebels: A Study of Master-Slave Relations in Antigua with Implications for Colonial British America.* Baltimore: Johns Hopkins University Press, 1985.

Gawthorp, Humphrey. 'George Ellis of Ellis Caymanas: A Caribbean Link to Scott and the Bronte Sisters.' *Electronic British Library Journal* (2005). Accessed 22 October 2021, https://www.bl.uk/eblj/2005articles/article3.html

Ghirelli, Michael. *A List of Emigrants from England to America, 1682–1692.* Baltimore: Genealogical Publishing Company, 1989.

Great Britain. Public Record Office. *Calendar of State Papers, Domestic Series, of the Reign of Charles I: 1631–1633.* London: Longman, Brown, Green, Longmans, and Roberts, 1862.

Haasse, W.H.J. *Annear Family History: 1813–1976.* [np]: Haasse, 1990. Accessed 8 November 2022, https:www.haasse-ea.info

Hall, Catherine. 'The Slavery Business and the Making of "Race" in Britain and the Caribbean.' *Current Anthropology.* (Vol.61, Supplement 22, October 2020).

Hays, Mary. *The Victim of Prejudice.* 2nd ed. Peterborough: Broadview Press, 1998.

Henderson, James. 'On the Methods Generally Adopted in Cornwall in Dressing Tin and Copper Ore; With Abstracts of the Discussions.' In *Minutes of the Proceedings of the Institution of Civil Engineers* Vol.17, pp.195–212. London: Institution of Civil Engineers, 1858.

Henwood, George. *Cornwall's Mines and Miners: Nineteenth Century Studies.* Truro: Bradford Barton, 1972. (First published in the *Mining Journal* between June 1857 and May 1859 under the title 'Cornish Mine Photographs and Cornish Mining Maxims'.)

Hotten, John Camden. *The Original List of Persons of Quality: Emigrants, Religious Exiles, Political Rebels. Serving Men Sold for a Term of Years, Apprentices, Children Stolen, Maidens Pressed, and Others. Who went from Great Britain to the American Plantations, 1600–1700.* London: Empire State Book Company, 1874. Accessed August 2021, https://babel.hathitrust.org/cgi/pt?id=mdp.39015003632877&view=1up&seq=9&skin=2021

Howard, Robert Mowbray. 'Edward Long's Sisters.' In *Records and Letters of the Family of the Longs of Longville, Jamaica, and Hampton Lodge, Surrey*, pp.183–196. London: Simpkin, Marshall, Hamilton, Kent and Co., 1925.

Hunt, Gerard M. *Desperate in Saint Martin: Notes on Guillaume Coppier*. Bloomington: Trafford Publishing, 2013

Immel, Andrea. *An Enslaved Woman Learns to Read in Eliza Fenwick's A Visit to the Juvenile Library (1805)*. Accessed 12 September 2022, https://blogs.princeton.edu/cotsen/tag/enslaved-people/

Jamaica: Addresses to His Excellency Edward John Eyre, Esquire, 1865, 1866. [Kingston]: M de Cordova and Company, 1866. Accessed 2 August 2022, https://archive.org/stream/jamaicaaddresse00eyregoog/jamaicaaddresse00eyregoog_djvu.txt

Jamaica Almanacs. Accessed throughout 2021, http://www.jamaicanfamilysearch.com/Samples/Almanacs.htm

Jeaffreson, Christopher. *A Young Squire of the Seventeenth Century: From the Papers (A.D. 1676–1686) of Christopher Jeaffreson*. London: Hurst and Blackett, 1876. Accessed September 2021, https://books.google.com.ag/books?id=P2sxAQAAMAAJ&vq=servants&dq=17+century+squire+st+christopher+sugar+plantation&source=gbs_navlinks_s

Johnson, Howard and Karl Watson, eds. *The White Minority in the Caribbean*. Kingston: Ian Randle, 2000

John Price of Penzance, the Elder: Profile & Legacies Summary 1712–1740. Accessed 1 October 2021, https://www.ucl.ac.uk/lbs/person/view/2146640647

Jones, Cecily. 'Contesting the Boundaries of Gender, Race and Sexuality in Barbadian Plantation Society.' *Women's History Review*, pp. 195–232 (Vol.12, No.2, 2003)

Jones, Cecily. *Engendering Whiteness: White Women and Colonialism in Barbados and North Carolina, 1627–1865*. Manchester: Manchester University Press, 2014.

Kaminkow, Marion. *A List of Emigrants from England to America, 1718–1759*. Baltimore: Genealogical Publishing Company, 1989.

Lane, C. 'Travellers and the Industrial Revolution: Observations of Cornwall.'

Hons diss., Edith Cowan University, 2002. Accessed 7 May 2021, https://ro.ecu.edu.au/theses_hons/540

Legacies of British Slave Ownership. Accessed throughout 2021 and 2022, https://www.ucl.ac.uk/lbs/

Legacies of British Slave Ownership: Estates. Accessed 1 April 2022, https://www.ucl.ac.uk/lbs/estates/

Leifchild, J.R. *Cornwall: its Mines and Miners; With Sketches of Scenery.* 2nd Ed. London: Longman, Brown Green, 1857.

Lemon, Charles. 'The Statistics of the Copper Mines of Cornwall.' *Journal of the Statistical Society of London,* pp.65–84 (Vol.1, No.2, June 1838).

Letter of P.J. Minvielle to Julius Price, 22 April 1847, St Thomas, Virgin Islands. Baring Archive. HC5 5.13.1 1847.

'Letters from Barbados'. *The Royal Gazette: Bermuda Commercial and General Advertiser and Recorder.* (Vol.57, 23 August 1881).

Letters from Christopher Bethel Codrington to John James [and family]. Gloucestershire Records Office, D1610 C24. Accessed 29 August 2022, https://digital.lib.sfu.ca/cwc-97/letters-christopher-bethell-codrington-john-james?search=John%2520James

Ligon, Richard and Karen Ordahl Kupperman. *The True and Exact History of the Island of Barbados.* Cambridge: Hacket Publishing Company, 2011. First published in 1657.

Long, Edward. *The History of Jamaica or, General Survey of the Antient and Modern State of that Island: with Reflections on its Situation, Settlements, Inhabitants, Climate, Products, Commerce, Laws, and Government.* London: T. Lowndes, 1774. Accessed October 2021, https://repository.library.northeastern.edu/downloads/neu:m0410b06w?datastream_id=content

Luffman, John. *A Brief Account of the Island of Antigua, Together with the Customs and Manners of its Inhabitants, as well White as Black ...* 2nd ed. Rev. Farmington Hills: Gale, 2010.

Lynch, Theodora Elizabeth. *Years Ago: A Tale of West Indian Domestic Life of the Eighteenth Century.* London: Jarrold and Sons, 1865.

MacKenzie, Charlotte. *Cornish Connections with 1790s Radical and Literary*

Circles: Part 1. Accessed 24 September 2021, http://cornishstory.com/2019/04/07/cornish-connections-with-1790s-radical-and-literary-circles/

MacKenzie, Charlotte. *Women Writers and Georgian Cornwall*. Truro: Cornwall History, 2020.

Mair, Lucille Mathurin. *A Historical Study of Women in Jamaica: 1655–1844*. Kingston: University of the West Indies Press, 2006.

Manktelow, Emily. *Missionary Families: Race, Gender and Generation on the Spiritual Frontier*. Manchester: Manchester University Press, 2016.

Martínez-Fernández, Luis. ' "Don't Die Here": the Death and Burial of Protestants in the Hispanic Caribbean, 1840–1885.' *The Americas*, pp.23–47 (Vol.49, No.1, July 1992).

Mayers, Lynne. *A Dangerous Place to Work*. Cinderford: Blaize Bailey Books, 2008.

Mayers, Lynne. *Balmaidens*. Penzance: Hypatia Press, 2004.

Mayers, Lynne. *The St Austell Bal Maidens: Women and Girls at the Mines and Clay Works*. Cinderford: Blaize Bailey Books, 2011.

Methodist Missionary Society Handlists. Accessed 1 November 2022, https://digital.soas.ac.uk/AA00001361/00009/19x.

Methodist Who's Who 1912. London: Kelly, nd.

Minutes of the Methodist Conferences. Vol. XI. London: John Mason, 1852.

Moister, William. *Memorials of Missionary Labours in Western Africa and the West Indies …* 3rd ed., London: [Wesleyan Conference Office], 1850, p.324.

Moore, Brian L., B.W. Higman, Carl Campbell and Patrick Bryan (eds.) *Slavery, Freedom and Gender: The Dynamics of Caribbean Society*. Kingston: University of the West Indies Press, 2003.

Moore Hall, Jamaica, St Mary: Estate Details. Accessed 18 October 2021, https://www.ucl.ac.uk/lbs/estate/view/2526

Morrissey, Marietta. *Slave Women in the New World: Gender Stratification in the Caribbean*. Lawrence: University Press of Kansas, 1989.

Neal, John. *'In the Beginning…' Gender, Ethnicity and the Methodist Missionary Enterprise*. Accessed 4 April 2021, missionary-history-neal-in-the-beginning-2011.pdf

Nugent, Maria, Lady. *Lady Nugent's Journal: Jamaica One Hundred and Thirty-Eight Years Ago*. Edited by Frank Cundall. London: West India Committee for the Institute of Jamaica, 1939.

O'Callaghan, Evelyn. *Women Writing the West Indies, 1804–1939: 'A Hot Place, Belonging to Us'*. London: Routledge, 2004.

Olwig, Karen Fog. 'The Struggle for Respectability: Methodism and Afro-Caribbean Culture on Nineteenth Century Nevis'. *Nieuwe West-Indische Gidsl New West Indian Guide*. (Vol.64, Nos.3 and 4, 1990), pp.93–114.

Parker, Matthew. *The Sugar Barons*. London: Windmill Books, 2012.

Parsons, Jack, and Nora Parsons. *Cornish Fisherboy to Master Mariner: The Life of Henry Blewett 1836–1891. Part One 1836–1861: Mousehole Boyhood and Early Days at Sea*. Bournemouth: Bournemouth Local Studies Publications, 1993.

Parsons, Jack, and Nora Parsons. *Cornish Fisherboy to Master Mariner: The Life of Henry Blewett 1836–1891. Part Two 1861–1866: Mate and Master Mariner*. Bournemouth: Bournemouth Local Studies Publications, 1993.

Parsons, Jack, and Nora Parsons. *Cornish Fisherboy to Master Mariner: The Life of Henry Blewett 1836–1891. Part Three 1866–1881: Roseau Days*. Bournemouth: Bournemouth Local Studies Publications, 1994.

Paul, Lissa. *Eliza Fenwick: Early Modern Feminist*. Newark: University of Delaware Press, 2019.

Paul, Lissa. 'How Barbados Transformed Radical British Author Eliza Fenwick into a Reactionary.' In *Caribbean Literature in Transition, 1800–1920*, edited by Evelyn O'Callaghan and Tim Watson, pp.151–67. Caribbean Literature in Transition. Cambridge: Cambridge University Press, 2021.

Payton, Philip. 'Bal Maidens and Cousin Jenny: The Paradox of Women in Australia's Historic Mining Communities.' In *Australia, Migration and Empire: Immigrants in a Globalised World*, edited by Philip Payton and Andrekos Varnava, pp.207–228. Cham: Palgrave Macmillan, 2019.

Payton, Philip. *The Cornish Overseas: A History of Cornwall's 'Great Emigration'.* Exeter: University of Exeter Press, 2020.

Perez del Castillo, Guillermo. 'The Harvey Family in El Cobre.' *Revista: Cuban Genealogical Society,* pp.2–4 (Vol.15, January 2006).

Pigot's Directory of Cornwall, 1830. Accessed 15 March 2021, http://specialcollections.le.ac.uk/digital/collection/p16445coll4/id/64257/

Polsue, Joseph. *A Complete Parochial History of the County of Cornwall.* Vol.2. Truro: William Lake, 1868.

Pritchard, John. *Methodist Women Abroad: Roles and Relationships.* Accessed 25 April 2021, methodistheritage.org.uk/missionary-history-pritchard-methodist-women-abrod02011.pdf.

Prykhodko, Yaroslav. 'The Social Life of Edward Long.' In 'Mind, Body, and the Moral Imagination in the Eighteenth-Century British Atlantic World.' PhD diss., University of Pennsylvania, 2011. Accessed 8 October 2021, https://repository.upenn.edu/cgi/viewcontent.cgi?article=1719&context=edissertations

Rebovich, Samantha Anne. 'Landscape, Labour, and Practice: Slavery and Freedom at Green Castle Estate, Antigua.' PhD diss., Syracuse University, 2011. Accessed 20 January 2021, https://core.ac.uk/download/pdf/215701612.pdf.

Redding, Cyrus. *Fifty Years' Reflections, Literary and Personal, with Observations on Men and Things.* Vol.1. London: Charles J. Skeete, 1858. Accessed 3 November 2021, https://lordbyron.org/monograph.php?doc=CyReddi.1858&select=ContentsI

Rosenthal, Jamie. 'From Radical Feminist to Caribbean Slave Owner: Eliza Fenwick's Barbados Letters.' *Eighteenth-Century Studies,* pp.47–68 (Vol.52, No. 1, 2018).

Rosenthal, Jamie. 'Of Bonds and Bondage: Gender, Slavery, and Transatlantic Intimacies in the Eighteenth Century.' PhD diss., University of California, San Diego, 2012. Accessed 30 August 2022, https://escholarship.org/uc/item/652486x7.

Ross, Cathy. *'Without Faces':* Women's Perspectives on Contextual Missiology. Accessed 12 March 2021, methodistheritage.org.uk/missionary-history-ross-without-faces-2011.pdf.

Sacks, David Harris. *The Widening Gate: Bristol and the Atlantic Economy, 1450–1700*. Berkeley: University of California Press, 1991.

Samuel Long of Tredudwell: Profile & Legacies Summary. Accessed 12 October 2021, https://www.ucl.ac.uk/lbs/person/view/2146633746

Schaw, Janet. *Journal of a Lady of Quality: Being the Narrative of a Journey from Scotland to the West Indies, North Carolina and Portugal, in the Years 1774 to 1776*. Edited by Evangeline Walker Andrew in collaboration with Charles McLain Andrews. New Haven: University of Yale Press, 1921.

Schwartz, Sharron P. *The Cornish in Latin America: 'Cousin Jack' and the New World*. Wicklow: Cornubian Press, 2016.

Seaborn, R Laurel. 'Seafaring Women: An Investigation of Material Culture for Potential Archaeological Diagnostics of Women on Nineteenth-Century Sailing Ships.' Master's thesis, East Carolina University, 2014. Accessed 7 October 2022, https://thescholarship.ecu.edu/bitstream/handle/10342/4535/Seaborn_ecu_0600O_11155.pdf?sequence=1&isAllowed=y

Sears, Minerva. *Journal of the Captain's Wife: An 1852 Voyage from Calcutta to Boston*; transcribed and edited by Matthew McKnight. Diary File, 2017.

Seville Heritage Park. Accessed 25 October 2021, https://whc.unesco.org/en/tentativelists/5431.

Shepherd, Verene, Bridget Brereton and Barbara Bailey (eds). *Engendering Caribbean History: Cross-Cultural Perspectives*. Kingston, Ian Randle, 2011.

Shepherd, Verene (ed.) *Women in Caribbean History*. Kingston: Ian Randle, 2012.

Smith, Robert Emerson. *Colonists in Bondage: White Servitude and Convict Labor in America, 1607–1776*, p.228. Chapel Hill: University of North Carolina Press, 1947.

Sparrow, Elizabeth. *The Prices of Penzance: The Influence of 18th Century Jamaican Sugar Plantation Owners on West Cornwall*. Penzance: Sparrow, 1984.

Suranyi, Anna. *Indentured Servitude: Unfree Labour and Citizenship in the British Colonies*. Montreal: McGill-Queen's University Press, 2021.

Suranyi, Anna. 'Willing to Go if They Had Their Clothes: Early Modern Women and Indentured Servitude.' In *Challenging Orthodoxies: The Social and Cultural Worlds of Early Modern Women; Essays Presented to Hilda L. Smith*, edited by Sigrun Haude and Melinda S. Zook, pp.193–210. Abingdon: Routledge, 2016.

Symons, Maxine. 'Bring up the Bodies: Digging up the Truth in the Lost Mausoleum at Crowan.' *Journal of the Royal Institution of Cornwall*, pp.10–33 (2021).

Taylor, Becky. 'Immigration, Statecraft and Public Health: The 1920 Aliens Order, Medical Examinations and the Limitations of the State in England.' *Social History of Medicine*, pp.512–533 (Vol.29, No.3, 2016).

Taylor, John and David Buisseret. *Jamaica in 1687: The Taylor Manuscript at the National Library of Jamaica*. Kingston: University of the West Indies Press, 2008.

The Letters of John James Esq.: A Collection of Letters Written by the Estate Manager of Barbuda and Clare Hall, Antigua 1804–1826. Accessed 11 February 2022, http://johnjamesesq.blogspot.com/p/blog-page_2030.html

The National Archives of the UK. Public Record Office. *Census Returns of England and Wales, 1851, Charles Tillar*; Class: H0107; Piece: 1905; Folio: 28; Page: 16: GSU roll: 221057.

The National Archives of the UK. Public Record Office. *Census Returns of England and Wales, 1861, Charles Tillar*; Class: RG 9; Piece: 1527; Folio: 27; Page 21; GSU roll: 542826.

The National Archives of the UK. Public Record Office. *Census Returns of England and Wales, 1861. Mary Annear*. Class: RG 9; Piece: 1558; Folio: 49; Page: 23; GSU roll: 542831.

The National Archives of the UK. Public Record Office. *Census Returns of England and Wales, 1871. Jane Hodge*. Class: RG10; Piece: 2331; Folio: 36; Page: 16; GSU roll: 838828.

The National Archives of the UK. Public Record Office. *Census Returns of*

England and Wales, 1911. Elizabeth Ann Kernick. Class: RG 14; Piece: 16540; Page 132.

The National Archives of the UK. Public Record Office. *High Court of Admiralty: Prize Court: Registers of Declarations for Letters of Marque. HCA26/6/123.*

The National Archives of the UK. Public Record Office. *Records of the Prerogative Court of Canterbury: Will of Elizabeth James, Widow of Marazion, Cornwall*. PROB 11/1742/159.

The Register of Blundell's School Part 1: The Register 1770–1882. Exeter: J.G. Commin, 1904. Accessed 7 March 2022, https://forgottenbooks.com/it/download/TheRegisterofBlundellsSchool_10913062.pdf

'The Revd. William Lanyon Bennett …' *Saint Christopher Advertiser and Weekly Intelligencer*. p.4. (Tuesday 15 May 1883).

'To be Let …' *Royal Cornwall Gazette*, p.1. (Saturday 7 May 1817).

Traynor, Joanna. *The Slave Codes and Devon Men: A Significant Contribution*. Accessed 6 August 2021, https://www.ucl.ac.uk/lbs/media-new/pdfs/slavecodesanddevonmen.pdf

Trollope, Anthony. *The West Indies and the Spanish Main*. London, Chapman and Hall, 1860.

Trotter, Lesley. *The Married Widows of Cornwall: The Story of the Wives 'Left Behind' by Emigration*. St Day: Humble History Press, 2018.

Tweedy, Margaret T. 'A History of Barbuda Under the Codringtons 1738–1833.' PhD diss., University of Birmingham, 1981. Accessed 11 February 2022, https://etheses.bham.ac.uk/id/eprint/5356/

Virtual Jamestown. Registers of Servants Sent to Foreign Plantations. Bristol Registers 1654–1686. Accessed throughout August 2021, http://www.virtualjamestown.org/indentures/advsearch_bristol.html

Virtual Jamestown. Registers of Servants Sent to Foreign Plantations. London Registers 1682–1692. Accessed throughout August 2021, http://www.virtualjamestown.org/indentures/about_indentures.html#London1

Walker, Christine. 'Pursuing her Profits: Women in Jamaica, Atlantic Slavery and a Globalising Market, 1700–60.' *Gender and History*, pp.478–501 (Vol.26, No.3, November 2014).

Walker, Christine. 'Womanly Masters: Gendering Slave Ownership in Colonial Jamaica.' In *Women in Early America*, edited by Thomas A. Foster. (New York: New York University Press, 2015), pp.139–158.

Wareing, John. *Indentured Migration and the Servant Trade from London to America, 1618–1718: 'There is Great Want of Servants.'* Oxford: Oxford University Press, 2017.

Watters, David R. 'Observations on the Historic Sites and Archaeology of Barbuda.' *Journal of Archaeology and Anthropology*, pp.125–156 (Vol.3, No.2, 1980).

Watts, David. *The West Indies: Patterns of Development, Culture and Environmental Change Since 1492*. Cambridge: Cambridge University Press, 1987.

Whitburn, James. *A Cornish Man in Cuba: Transcript of a Diary of his Visit to Cuba 1836–1838*. np: Whitburn, nd. *William Trelawny – Burial – from the St Budeaux Parish Church Records*. National Library of Jamaica News Clipping File.

Williams, Eric. *From Columbus to Castro: The History of the Caribbean, 1492–1969*. New York: Vintage Books, 1984.

Wollstonecraft, Mary. *Maria: Or, the Wrongs of Woman*. New York: Norton, 1975.

Wollstonecraft, Mary. *A Vindication of the Rights of Woman*. Accessed 2 September 2022, https://www.gutenberg.org/ebooks/3420.

Wood, Betty. 'Servant Women and Sex in the Seventeenth-Century Chesapeake.' In *Women in Early America*, edited by Thomas A. Foster. (New York: New York University Press, 2015), pp.95–117.

Woodcock, Henry Iles. *A History of Tobago*. Ayr: Smith and Grant, 1867.

Wright Family: Jane Wright 1837–1921. Accessed 10 October 2022, http://www.mygenealogies.co.uk/Wright/WRIG-B3.htm

Young, Hannah. *Women, Slavery Compensation and Gender Relations in the 1830s*. London: University College London, nd. Accessed 20 January 2021, https://www.ucl.ac.uk/lbs/media-new/pdfs/hyoung.pdf.

Zacek, Natalie A. *Settler Society in the English Leeward Islands, 1670–1776*. New York: Cambridge University Press, 2010.

Zacek, Natalie. 'Searching for the Invisible Woman: The Evolution of

White Women's Experience in Britain's West Indian Colonies.' *History Compass*, pp.329–341 (Vol.7, No.1, 2009).

Zacek, Natalie and Laurence Brown. 'Unsettled Houses: The Material Culture of the Missionary Project in Jamaica in the Era of Emancipation.' *Slavery and Abolition*, pp.493–507 (Vol.35, No.3, 2014).

Zook, Melinda S. *Challenging Orthodoxies: The Social and Cultural Worlds of Early Modern Women*. London: Routledge, 2016.

Index

In this Index, females are indexed under their maiden surname, with a cross reference from their married surname.

Abaco, 100, 102, 103
   see also Bahamas
Allen, Ralph, 43-44
Anglicans, 50, 96, 107
Annear, Emma, 10
Annear, Mary Ann, 102
Annear, Samuel, 99-100, 103-104
Antigua, 3, 13, 48, 58, 62, 63, 64, 65, 92, 104-105, 107, 109, 123
   see also Barbuda
Apprenticeship system (for the formerly enslaved, following the Emancipation Act), 21, 47-48
Australia, 134, 137, 138
Ayres, Elizabeth, 20

Badcock, Henry, 23
Badcock, Parthesia *see* Keigwin, Parthesia
Badcock, Margery, 23-27, 55
Bahamas, 99-102
   see also Abaco

Bailey, Annie
   see Whitburn, Annie
Bailey, Edith, 107
Bailey, Ellen Annie, 107, 108
Bailey, Ernest, 107
Bailey, Herbert, 107
Bailey, Reginald, 107
Bailey, Thomas, 107
Bailey, Thomas Henry, 106-108
Bailey, William, 108
Bal maidens, 115-123, 144
Baptists, 46, 52, 96, 97
Barbados, 3, 9, 13, 14, 19, 48, 58, 71-73, 75, 77-78, 92, 113
Barbuda, 48, 57-65
   see also Codrington Castle
          Codrington Village
Bath, 43-44
Beaton, Isabella, 103
Belain d'Esnambuc, Pierre, 6
Bennett, Clara Morley
   see James, Clara Morley

Bennett, Ellen Burrall, 109
Bennett, Emma Morley, 109
Bennett, Kate Lanyon, 109, 110
Bennett, Richard Stanley, 109
Bennett, Vivian Edmonds, 109
Bennett, William Lanyon, 109-110
Bermuda, 77
Bishop, Albert, 99
Bishop, Anne West
  see Savery, Anne West
Bissett, Mary, 37
Blewett, Charles Alexander, 80, 88
Blewett, Eliza Jane, 80
Blewett, Henry, 80-81, 87-88
Blewett, Henry Michael, 81, 85
Blewett, Jane
  see Wright, Jane
Blewett, Mary Wright, 80
Blewett, Rosea Henrietta, 80, 84
Bligh, Ada Theodosia, 50
Bligh, Frederick Cherburgh, 50
Bligh, Emily Matilda
  see East, Emily Matilda
Blue Mountains, Jamaica, 41, 45, 46, 50
Bogle, Paul, 52, 53
Bovey, Louisa, 121, 122, 125
Brammer, Elizabeth Williams, 27
Brammer, John, 27
Brazil, 47, 88
Bristol, 3, 17, 18, 20
British Guiana, 80
British Virgin Islands, 116, 118
  see also Virgin Gorda
Bryan, Elizabeth
  see Rodon, Elizabeth
Bryan, Mary Elizabeth Pennant, 54
Bryan, William Pennant, 54
Bryant, Annetta
  see Holman, Annetta
Bryant, Nicholas, 142
Bryant, Sydney Seymour, 142
Bucking, 119-120, 123
Budock Vean, Cornwall, 140
Bussa's Rebellion, 75

Camborne, 109, 135
Cassava bread, 8, 11-12
Catholic
  see Roman Catholic
Caymanas Estate, Jamaica, 33
Charlestown Mines, 118
Cherry Hill Estate, Jamaica, 52
Clare Hall Estate, Antigua, 63-64, 65, 67
Clowance Manor, Cornwall, 56, 64
Cobbing, 119, 120
Cobre Mines Consolidated Company
  see Compañía Consolidada de Minas del Cobre
Cocks, Ellen Mary
  see Savery, Ellen Mary
Cocks, John Edgar Wright, 113
Cocks, William, 99

INDEX

Cocks, William Francis, 87, 112-113
Codrington, Christopher Bethel, 57-59, 64, 65-66
Codrington Castle, 60-61
Codrington Village,, 60, 62-63, 64
Coke, Thomas, 92
Compañía Consolidada de Minas del Cobre, 128, 133
Compensation (to former owners of enslaved workers), 47, 48, 54
Coppier, Guillaume, 9-10, 11-12
Corfield, Bertha Elizabeth, 126
Corfield, Bessie, 126, 127
Corfield, Dora, 126, 127
Corfield, Emmaline, 126
Corfield, Richard Cecil, 126
Corfield, Thomas, 126
Corfield, Thomas Joseph, 126
Corporation of Trinity House, 89, 90
Coverture, 27, 55, 57, 66, 137
Creighton Estate, Jamaica, 45
Cromwell, Oliver, 5, 19, 28
Crowan, 56, 65, 135
Cuba, 47, 127-136, 138-143

Daniell, Anne, 44-54
Daniell, Elizabeth
 see Pooley, Elizabeth Mason
Daniell, Ralph Allen, 43-44, 52
Daniell, Thomas, 42-43, 52
Decoy Estate, Jamaica, 25
Dominica, 12, 80, 109-111

East, Anne
 see Daniell, Anne
East, Edward Hinton, 45, 52
East, Edward Hyde, 46, 48, 49
East, Emily Matilda, 49, 50
East, Francis Hyde, 49, 52
East, Hinton, 44-46, 52
East, Isabella Anne, 45, 51-52
East, Janetta Gertrude, 45, 50
East, John, 44-45
East, Mary Elizabeth, 45, 50
East Crinnis Mine, 118
Easter Rebellion
 see Bussa's Rebellion
El Cobre, 127-136, 138-141, 142-143
Ellis, Charles Rose, 33-34
Ellis, Charlotte
 see Long, Charlotte
Ellis, George, Junior, 32-33
Ellis, George, Senior, 32-33
Ellis, John, 33
Emancipation Act, 47-48, 79
Enslaved people, 3, 8, 9, 13-14, 16, 17, 19, 21, 25-27, 30-31, 32, 33, 46-48, 52, 54, 62, 70-71, 74-77, 79, 92-93, 122, 127-128, 130-131, 132, 144
Eyre, Edward John, 53

Falmouth, 18, 69, 106, 138
Fearon, Eliza Oakes, 54
Fearon, George Crawford Ricketts, 54

Fearon, Mary Burbury
    see McKenzie, Mary Burbury
Fenwick, Eliza Anne, 69, 71-73, 75, 77-78
Fenwick, Elizabeth
    see Jaco, Eliza
Fenwick, John, 68, 69
Fenwick, Orlando, 69, 73, 75
Fenwick, Thomas, 69
Fenwick, William Patrick, 73
Fowey, 28, 118
Fowey Consols, 118
Freedom dues, 15, 21
Froude, Anthony, 49-50

Gilbert, Nathaniel, 92
Godwin, William, 68
Gold Coast, West Africa, 99
Grateful Hill Methodist Mission, 91, 92, 93, 97, 98
Great Abaco see Abaco
Greencastle Estate, Jamaica, 32
Grenada, 36, 49-50
Guerra y Toledo, Dolores, 143
Guyana
    see British Guiana
Gwennap, 106, 112, 138, 139
Gwithian, 109

Haiti, 75
Hales, Emily, 87, 112-113
Hall, Emily
    see Hales, Emily
Hall, Irene Theodora, 113

Hall, Dorothea Greta, 113
Hall, Joseph, 113
Harvey, Albert, 143
Harvey, Carlos de Caridad, 143
Harvey, Frederick, 143
Harvey, Jane, junior, 142
Harvey, Jane, senior
    see Kemp, Jane
Harvey, John, 140, 143
Harvey, Josiah, 142
Harvey, Juliana, 142
Harvey, Theodore, 142
Harvey, William, 143
Hay, Mary, 68, 69, 73-74, 76, 77, 78
Hayle Foundry, 143
Heard, Fidelia, 83
Heming, Beeston Henry, 36
Heming, Elizabeth
    see Long, Elizabeth
Heming, Samuel, 34
Hemmings, Samuel, 34
Hen Frigate, 83
Henwood, George, 121, 122
Hicks, Edith Rosaline, 134
Hicks, Effie Evelyn, 134
Hicks, Elizabeth Jane, junior, 134
Hicks, Elizabeth Jane, senior
    see Johns, Elizabeth Jane
Hicks, William, junior, 134
Hicks, William, senior, 134
Hodge, Edward, 143
Hodge, Edwin, 143
Hodge, Ellen Jane, 143

INDEX

Hodge, Jane
  see Harvey, Jane, junior
Hodge, Maria, 143
Holcroft, Thomas, 68
Holman, Amelia
  see Pascoe, Amelia
Holman, Annetta, 141
Holman, Charles, 141, 142
Holman, Edwin, 142
Holman, Eliza, 141
Holman, Ellen, 141
Holman, James, 141
Holman, John, 141, 142
Holman, John James, 142
Holman, Julia, 141
Hurricanes, 35, 75, 78, 129, 132

Indenture, 3, 4, 7-8, 14, 15, 16, 17, 18, 21, 57
Indentured servants, 1-22, 122

Jaco, Eliza, 67-79, 89-90
Jaco, Peter, 68
Jamaica, 3, 11, 13, 19-20, 23-35, 37-46, 49-55, 91-99, 141-142
James, Clara Morley, 109-110
James, Elizabeth
  see Wingfield, Elizabeth
James, Elizabeth Prideaux, 57, 60, 67
James, John, 57-65
James, John Wingfield, 57, 60, 66
James, Mary, 57, 60, 62-63, 66-67
John, Elizabeth
  see Opie, Elizabeth
John, Mary, 137
John, Thomas, 137
Johns, Catherine, 134
Johns, Elizabeth Jane, 129, 134
Johns, Jane
  see Williams, Jane
Johns, Mary Ann, 129.
Johns, Zacharias, junior, 134
Johns, Zacharias, senior, 129, 133-134

Kalinago, 6, 8, 9, 11-12
Kea, 121
Keigwin, Parthesia, 23-24
Kemp, Jane, 142-143, 144
Kenwyn, 141
Kernick, Elizabeth Ann
  see Williams, Elizabeth Ann
Kernick, Frederick Walwyn, 105
Kernick, Henry Williams, 106
Kernick, John, 104-106
Kernick, Marion Grace, 106
Kingstown Methodist Mission, 112

'Ladies of Quality', 16, 23-55
Lamb, Charles, 68
Lamb, Mary, 68
Lanner, 142, 143
Ligon, Richard, 13
Lindsay, Charlotte
  see Long, Charlotte
Lindsay, David, 34

Lindsay, Elizabeth, 34
Lindsay, William, 34
Lisbon, Portugal, 88
Liskeard, 29, 126
Liverpool, 3, 136
London, 3, 4, 20, 27, 29, 34, 37, 55, 65, 66, 68, 70, 71, 80, 84, 85, 88, 92, 98, 99, 100, 101, 103, 104
Long, Catherine, 30-32
Long, Charles, 28
Long, Charlotte, 28-29, 32-34
Long, Edward, 31, 32, 35-36
Long, Edward Beeston, 32
Long, Elizabeth, 29-30, 34-36
Long, Mary
  see Tate, Mary.
Long, Robert, 28
Long, Samuel (1638-1683), 28
Long, Samuel (1700-1757), 28-30
Looe, 37, 44

Maclaverty, Colin, 50
Maclaverty, Mary Elizabeth
  see East, Mary Elizabeth
Madras, India, 88
Madron, 54, 55
Manderson, Elizabeth Ann, 138-140, 42-43
Mansion House, Truro, 43, 44
Marazion, 56, 57, 58, 59, 60, 62, 65
Marazion (merchant ship), 57
Marescaux, Isabella Anne
  see East, Isabella Anne

Marescaux, Oscar Adolphe Yeats, 51-52
Maryland Estate, Jamaica, 45, 48, 49, 52, 53
May, Catherine, 135
May, Charles, 135
May, John, 135
May, Richard, 134-135
May, Solomon Palmer, 135
May, Susan
  see Palmer, Susan
May, William, 135
McKenzie, Mary Burbury, 54
McKenny, Caroline, 136, 137
McKenny, Daniel, junior, 135, 136
McKenny, Daniel, senior, 135-136, 137
McKenny, Elizabeth
  see Opie, Elizabeth
McKenny, Elizabeth Marianne, 135, 138
McKenny, Isaac, 135, 138
McKenny, Jacob (born 1832, died in infancy), 135
McKenny, Jacob (born 1834), 135, 138
McKenny, Mary, 136, 137-138
McKenny, Samuel, 135, 138
McKenny, William, 139-140
Melrose, Andrew, 137
Melrose, Anne, 137
Melrose, Benjamin, 138
Melrose, Daniel Curtis, 138
Melrose, Elizabeth Mary, 137

INDEX

Melrose, Helen Caroline, 138
Melrose, James Alexander, 138
Melrose, Mary
  see McKenny, Mary
Melrose, William Harold, 138
Methodist chapels, 79, 86, 87, 93, 104-105, 112, 123
Methodist missionaries, 91-114
Methodist Missionary Society, 91, 95, 98, 99, 100, 101, 107, 129
Methodists, 87, 91-114, 123, 131
Michel, John, 54
Michel, Mary Elizabeth Pennant
  see Bryan, Mary Elizabeth Pennant
Mining, 115-144
Monmouth Rebellion, 5, 107
Moore Hall Estate, Jamaica, 32
Montserrat, 3, 107, 109
Moore, Charlotte
  see Long, Charlotte
Moore, Henry, 30-32
Moore, John Henry, 30, 32
Moore, Susanna Jane, 30, 32
Morant Bay Rebellion, 52-53
Moravians, 96
Mortimer, Elizabeth Prideaux
  see James, Elizabeth Prideaux
Mortimer, George, 67
Mortimer, William Bassett, 67
Mousehole, 79-80, 88

Nancarro, Ellin, 1-2, 6, 8, 10, 12-13, 17

Nassau Methodist Mission, 100, 102
Nevis, 3, 7, 18, 19, 104
New Haven, Connecticut, 77, 78
Newhaven, West Sussex, 108
New Sombrero Phosphate Company, 126
Newlyn, 68
Nicholls, Frank, 23
Nugent, Maria, 26, 38, 40, 41

Opie, Elizabeth, 135-137, 139

Palmer, Susan, 134-135
Par Consols, 118
Parkhoskin, 142
Pascoe, Amelia, 141-142
Pearce, Ellen Annie
  see Bailey, Ellen Annie
Pearce, Herbert, 108
Pearce, Mary Emma, 126
Pelynt, 37
Pender, Francis Henry, 140
Pender, Jane Abigail
  see Treweek, Jane Abigail
Penn, William, 28, 34, 45
Penryn, 2
Penwartha House, Cornwall
Penzance, 23, 24, 27, 54, 57, 62, 69, 70, 79, 137
Perranporth, 142
Perranzabuloe, 142
Plymouth, 1, 2, 3, 17, 20, 137
Plympton, 2

Pooley, Elizabeth Mason, 43-44
Price, Charles (1708-1739), 23, 24
Price, Charles Godolphin, 27
Price, Elizabeth
   see Brammer, Elizabeth Williams
Price, Francis, 28
Price, John, junior, 24, 27
Price, John, senior, 23-24
Price, Margery
   see Badcock, Margery
Price, Thomas Rose, 23, 24
Primitive Methodist Connection, 101
Prince, Mary, 77

Ragging, 119
Raymond Hall, Jamaica
Real de Santiago, 128, 132
Redruth, 99, 128, 129, 132, 133-134, 135-136, 137, 142
Robert Bonaventure (merchant ship), 1, 7, 8
Robinson, Crabb, 68
Rodin, Elinor, 17-19
Rodon, Elizabeth, 54
Rodon, Mary, 54
Roman Catholics, 107, 131, 139, 140, 141, 143
Rose Hall Estate, Jamaica, 25
Roseau (merchant ship), 81, 84, 85, 88, 112
Roselyon House, 28
Rotten boroughs, 37, 47

Rowland, Mary, 84-85
Royal Santiago Mining Company
   see Real de Santiago
Rutherford, Eliza Anne
   see Fenwick, Eliza Anne
Rutherford, William, 73, 76, 77

Sam Sharpe Rebellion, 46, 92
Sandy Point Methodist Mission, 106-107
Satchell, Agnes, 109-110
Savery, Ann West, 94, 99
Savery, Edith Mary, 98
Savery, Ellen Mary, 94, 99
Savery, George, 91-92, 98
Savery, George Mearns, 94
Savery, Philippa Ann
   see West, Philippa Ann
Savery, Samuel Servington, 98
Scruttons, 80, 81, 88
Sears, Minerva, 85-86
Seville Plantation, Jamaica, 34
Skeats, Mary Ann
   see Annear, Mary Ann
Smithett, Janetta Gertrude
   see East, Janetta Gertrude
Smithett, Marcus Edmiston, 50
Sombrero, 125-126
Sombrero Company, 125-126
Spalling, 119-120
St Agnes, 87, 112, 135
St Aubyn, Elizabeth
   see Wingfield, Elizabeth (wife of Sir John St Aubyn)

INDEX

St Austell, 28, 99, 117, 118, 121, 122
St Bart's
see Saint Barthélemy
St Barthélemy, 106
St Mawes, 138
St Michael's Mount, 56, 64
Sugar plantations, 9, 17, 18-19, 23-26, 28, 32-33, 35, 46-47, 54, 56, 58, 63, 75, 80, 88, 128, 130
St Breock, 91, 110
St Christopher, 1, 3, 6-7, 9, 13, 17, 18, 106-107, 109, 110, 113, 126, 127
St Kitts
see St Christopher
St Thomas, 124
St Vincent, 81, 82, 84, 85, 86, 87, 88, 112

Tacky's Rebellion, 30
Tate, Henry, 103
Tate, Mary, 28-30
Ten Years' War, Cuba, 133
'The Middling Sort', 46, 56-90, 96, 98, 103, 140
Thomas, Mary, 99-104
Tillar, Charles, 124
Tillar, Louise
see Bovey, Louise
Tillar, Elizabeth, 121, 124
Tillar, William, 121, 122, 125
Tobago, 58
Tredudwell, 28, 30

Tregony, 134
Trelawny, Anne, 38, 40-42
Trelawny, Harry, 37
Trelawny, Laetitia, junior, 37-42
Trelawny, Laetitia, senior, 37
Trelawny, Mary
see Bissett, Mary
Trelawny, William, junior, 37, 38, 42
Trelawny, William, senior, 37
Trelissick Estate, Cornwall, 44-45
Trinidad, 50
Treweek, Ann Curgenven, 140
Treweek, Elizabeth Ann, senior
see Manderson, Elizabeth Ann
Treweek, Elizabeth Ann, junior, 139, 140
Treweek, Francis, 139
Treweek, George Manderson, 140
Treweek, James, 138, 140
Treweek, James Manderson, 138
Treweek, Jane Abigail, 139, 140
Treweek, John Henry Martin, 138
Treweek, Nicholas, 139
Treweek, William Tiddy, 139
Trewin, Jane, 1-2, 6, 8, 10, 12-13, 17
Trollope, Anthony, 49
Truro, 42-44, 54, 103, 113, 141, 142
Tuckingmill, 135
Tywardreath, 121, 135

Venables, Robert, 28, 34, 45

Veryan, 134
Virgin Gorda, 116-125
Virgin Gorda Mining Company, 117, 121-125
Vincent, Richard, 32
Vincent, George, 18

Wadebridge, 110
Walcott, John, 38, 41-42
Warner, Thomas, 6, 18
Wesley, John, 68, 92, 94, 106
Wesleyan Methodists
  see Methodists
West, Elizabeth Ann
  see Treweek, Elizabeth Ann
West, Philippa Ann, 91-94, 98
West, Thomas, 140
West Norwood Cemetery, 103-104
Whitburn, Annie, 106-108

Wilce, Annetta
  see Holman, Annetta
Wilce, Leonard, 142
Wilce, Luke, 142
Williams, Elizabeth Ann, 104, 105-106
Williams, Jane, 129-131, 133-134
Williams, Jenifer
  see Williams, Jane
Wingfield, Elizabeth, 56-67, 89-90
Wingfield, Elizabeth (wife of Sir John St Aubyn), 56
Wingfield, George, 56
Wollstonecraft, Mary, 68, 69
Worthy Park Estate, Jamaica, 24, 26, 27, 55
Wright, Jane, 79-90

Yellow fever, 8, 41-42, 75, 110, 113, 127, 130

This book is printed on paper from sustainable sources managed under the Forest Stewardship Council (FSC) scheme.

It has been printed in the UK to reduce transportation miles and their impact upon the environment.

For every new title that Troubador publishes, we plant a tree to offset CO_2, partnering with the More Trees scheme.

MORE TREES
LET'S PLANT A BILLION TREES

For more about how Troubador offsets its environmental impact, see www.troubador.co.uk/sustainability-and-community